# Safeguard Your F&B Empire

# Safeguard Your F&B Empire

AKSHIT GUPTA

Worldwide Published by
 **Pendown** Press

**PENDOWN PRESS**

An ISO 9001 & ISO 14001 Certified Co.,

**Regd. Office:** 2525/193, 1st Floor, Onkar Nagar-A, Tri Nagar, Delhi-110035

**Ph.:** 09350849407, 09312235086

**E-mail:** info@pendownpress.com

**Branch Office:** 1A/2A, 20, Hari Sadan, Ansari Road, Daryaganj, New Delhi-110002

**Ph.:** 011-45794768

**Website:** PendownPress.com

**First Edition:** 2023

**ISBN:** 978-93-5554-525-1



*Layout and Cover Designed by* Pendown Graphics Team

*Printed and Bound in India by* Thomson Press India Ltd.

# Dedication

---

Dedicated to my loving wife, Kavya, and my precious child, Arin,

To my wife, Kavya, you are my everything. Your love, support, and encouragement have been the driving force behind my every success. Your wisdom, kindness, and strength have been an endless source of inspiration to me. Your unwavering belief in me has been a constant reminder of how lucky I am to have you by my side.

To my child, Arin, you are the light of my life. Your innocence, curiosity, and joy have brought so much happiness to my heart. Watching you grow and learn has been a privilege, and I am grateful for every moment we spend together.

This book is a tribute to the love and life we have built together.

Forever and always,

~Akshit Gupta

# Contents

# Acknowledgements

First and foremost, I would like to express my deepest gratitude to my father, Shiv Gupta, who has been my mentor, guide, and role model throughout my life. Your unwavering support and encouragement have been instrumental in shaping the person I am today. Your wisdom and guidance have inspired me to reach for the stars, and your love and belief in me have given me the confidence to chase my dreams.

I would also like to extend my heartfelt thanks to my mother, Babita Gupta, for her love, care, and support. Your sacrifices and devotion to our family have been a constant source of inspiration, and your encouragement and understanding have been a beacon of hope during the toughest times.

I am also grateful to my family, friends, teachers, and colleagues, who have supported and inspired me throughout my journey. Your guidance, advice, and encouragement have been invaluable, and I am thankful for the meaningful relationships that we have built together.

Finally, I would like to express my gratitude to the team at Asha Ram & Sons, for their support and guidance in bringing this book to life. Their expertise, professionalism, and dedication have been instrumental in helping me bring my vision to life.

Thank you all for being a part of my journey and for making this book possible.

With love and gratitude,

~Akshit Gupta

# Foreword

It is my pleasure to introduce this remarkable book by Akshit Gupta. As a fellow friend and strategic business partner, I have had the privilege of witnessing Akshit's growth and development as a writer, and I can say with confidence that this book is a testament to his passion, talent, and dedication to his craft.

If you are in the food and beverage industry, you know how challenging it can be to run a successful business while managing costs effectively. In "Safeguard your F&B Empire," Akshit provides you with a wealth of knowledge and expertise on how to tackle the cost-saving challenges faced by industry professionals. This book offers practical advice and valuable insights on topics such as forex hedging, contract timing, and navigating market fluctuations. The author also provides guidance on how to choose the right partner, conduct financial checks, and manage supply chain disruptions during a pandemic.

Whether you are a seasoned professional or just starting out in the food industry, this book is a must-read for anyone looking to improve their ingredient purchasing skills and safeguard their business against the common mistakes made by 90% of buyers in the industry. With its comprehensive approach and wealth of knowledge, "Safeguard your F&B Empire" provides the tools you need to make informed purchasing decisions, negotiate better deals, and maintain a stable and consistent supply chain. So, if you're looking to innovate and grow your food and beverage business, be sure to add this book to your library today!

Regards

~Tom Munro

*Sales Manager - Indian Subcontinent*
*Fonterra Co-operative Group Limited*

# Foreword

I am really honoured to introduce this book and delighted to present Akshit Gupta's remarkable book. I have had the privilege of watching Akshit's growth as a writer. This book is a testament to his passion, talent, and dedication to his craft. I have had the privilege of reviewing this manuscript and I can confidently say that it offers a valuable contribution to the field of the Food & Beverage Industry. As a strategic business partner for more than 12 years and a dear friend, Akshit's thorough research, insightful analysis, and engaging writing style make this book a must-read for anyone interested in the topic. He has demonstrated their ability to provide clear and concise explanations of complex concepts, making them accessible to a wide range of readers. I am proud to be associated with this work and I believe it will be an influential and inspiring addition to the book.

Through the pages of this book, you will gain a comprehensive understanding of the topic, which is presented in a logical and engaging manner.

In "Safeguard Your F&B Empire," Akshit shares his expertise in managing costs and tackling cost-saving challenges in the food and beverage industry. Akshit's use of real-world examples, case studies, and practical applications make this book an invaluable resource for both business professionals and novices alike.

Throughout the pages of "Safeguard Your F&B Empire", Akshit demonstrates a deep knowledge of improving ingredient purchasing skills and safeguarding their business against common mistakes, as well as a gift for clear and concise writing. The insights presented here are sure to challenge readers and spark new ideas and conversations.

I hope that you will find this book as informative , useful  and enjoyable

Regards

**~Sham Gambhire**

*M.Tech (Food Science)*
*Director, Royal Ingredients India*

# About the Book

Are you tired of making costly mistakes when buying food ingredients? Do you want to avoid the pitfalls that 90% of buyers fall into when purchasing these essentials? Look no further. In this comprehensive guide, you will learn about the seven most common mistakes buyers make and how to fix them permanently.

The author delves into topics such as forex hedging, contract timing, and how to navigate bull and bear market scenarios. They also provide insights on how to choose the right partner, whether it's a multinational corporation or an owner-driven company, and the importance of conducting thorough financial checks. The book also covers the challenges posed by supply chain disruptions during a pandemic and the advantages & disadvantages of implementing an L1, L2, and L3 strategy.

With its practical advice and expert insights, this book will equip you with the knowledge and skills you need to make informed decisions when purchasing food ingredients. Whether you're a seasoned professional or just starting out, you'll learn how to avoid common mistakes, negotiate better deals, and ensure a stable and consistent supply chain.

Don't wait to start your journey to smarter, more effective food ingredient purchasing. Grab a copy of "Safeguard your F&B Empire" today!

# Author Bio

$A$kshit is a certified Bakery Technologist, Dairy Science professional, and a food ingredients expert with a wealth of experience in the industry. With a strong background in business automation, Akshit is a lead strategist and has a proven track record of delivering results.

Education & Qualifications:

- Graduate in Bakery Science and Technology from American Institute of Baking (AIB), USA

- Diploma in Dairy Ingredient Technology from Center for Dairy Research (CDR), U.S.A.

- Graduation in Bcom (Hons) from Khalsa, Delhi University

- Master's Degree in Family business management from S.P. Jain Institute of Management & Research

- Diploma holder in Import-Export Management from International Trade Promotion Centre (ITPC)

- Learned organizational leadership from LSE, London School of Economics

- Multiple certifications in the field of bringing Technology & Automation in any business

- Development knowledge in Power BI Tool which is Integrate with SQL

- Master's in Advanced Sales and Marketing Strategies

- Expert in Automating Business Operations

- Expert knowledge in functionality of Bakery Ingredients

- Expert knowledge in Food Safety & Standard practices

- Knowledge in Sanitising & Good manufacturing practices (GMP)

- Certificate holder in Dairy Processing & Cheese Fundamentals

Personal Information:

- 4th generation entrepreneur in Asha Ram & Sons.

- 12+ years of experience in researching, formulating, and distributing new food ingredients across various food areas and demographics.

- Worked with over 2500 businesses and helped them grow their profits anywhere from 17% to over 200%

Throughout his career, Akshit has consistently demonstrated his commitment to excellence and his ability to drive innovation in the food industry. With his extensive knowledge of food ingredients, quality control, and supply chain management, he is well-positioned to help businesses achieve their goals.

Akshit's passion for the food industry and his drive to make a positive impact on the world are evident in everything he does. Through his writing and consulting work, he is dedicated to sharing his insights and expertise with others, empowering them to make informed decisions and achieve success in their own careers.

Whether you're a professional in the food industry, a student of food science, or simply someone with a passion for great food, Akshit's insights and expertise are sure to be of great value to you.

~Akshit Gupta

# Who should read this book?

This book is ideal for a wide range of professionals and individuals in the food industry, including:

Food Ingredients buyers: If you're responsible for purchasing food ingredients, this book is a must-read. You'll learn about the common mistakes buyers make and how to avoid them.

**Supply chain managers:** If you're responsible for managing a food ingredient supply chain, this book will provide you with the tools and strategies you need to ensure a stable and consistent supply.

**Research and Development professionals:** If you're part of an R&D team that is responsible for developing new food products or improving existing ones, this book will provide you with insights and best practices for sourcing **high-quality ingredients.**

**Quality control specialists:** If you're part of an R&D team that is responsible for ensuring the quality of food products, this book will provide you with the tools and strategies you need to make informed decisions about purchasing food ingredients.

**Food scientists and technologists:** If you're a food scientist or technologist, this book will provide you with a valuable understanding of the food ingredient purchasing process and help you ensure that your team is sourcing the highest-quality ingredients.

New product development teams: If you're part of a team responsible for developing new food products, this book will help you understand the mistakes that many buyers make and provide you with the strategies you need to avoid them.

This book is also ideal for anyone with an interest in the food industry and the processes that go into sourcing and purchasing food ingredients. With its practical advice and expert insights, it's the perfect resource for anyone looking to improve their understanding of the food ingredient purchasing process.

# How to use this book?

This book is designed to be a practical and actionable guide to help you avoid the common mistakes that many buyers make when purchasing food ingredients. Here's how to get the most out of this book:

**Read each chapter:** Each chapter of this book focuses on one of the seven common mistakes that buyers make when purchasing food ingredients. Read each chapter carefully to understand the mistake and how to avoid it.

**Take notes:** As you read each chapter, take notes on the key points and strategies. This will help you to remember the information and implement it in your own purchasing process.

**Reflect on your own practices:** As you read each chapter, reflect on your own food ingredient purchasing process. Are there any mistakes that you have made or are making? How can you avoid them in the future?

Apply the strategies: The final chapter of this book provides a summary of the strategies you can use to avoid the seven common mistakes. Take the time to read through these strategies and apply them to your own food ingredient purchasing process.

Share the book with your team: If you're part of an R&D team or procurement team, consider sharing this book with your colleagues. This will help you to ensure that everyone on your team is using best practices when it comes to purchasing food ingredients.

By following these steps, you will be able to use this book to improve your understanding of the food ingredient purchasing process and ensure that you are sourcing high-quality ingredients for your food products.

# Preface

As a seasoned professional in the food industry, I have seen first-hand the struggles that many buyers face when purchasing food ingredients. Over the years, I have encountered countless individuals who were making costly mistakes that could have been easily avoided. These mistakes often resulted in subpar ingredients, delayed product launches, and decreased profitability.

I realized that these mistakes were not due to a lack of knowledge or skill, but rather a lack of understanding of the basics and fundamentals of the food ingredient purchasing process. This realization led me to write this book, with the goal of educating my industry peers and helping them to avoid the common mistakes that many buyers make when purchasing food ingredients.

In this book, I cover the most common mistakes that buyers make, and provide practical and actionable strategies to help you avoid them. From understanding the importance of financial due diligence to developing a robust supply chain strategy, I provide the essential information and tools you need to make informed decisions when purchasing food ingredients.

I wrote this book because I wish there had been a resource like this available when I was entering in my business. I believe that by educating yourself on the basics and fundamentals of the food ingredient purchasing process, you can avoid the common mistakes and ensure that you are sourcing high-quality ingredients for your food products.

Whether you are a seasoned professional in the food industry or just starting out, this book is for you. I hope that it will serve as a valuable resource and help you to achieve your goals in the food industry.

# The Beginning

Akshit was always passionate about food, and after completing his graduation in Bakery Science and Technology from the American Institute of Baking (AIB), he was offered a handsome package to work in the United States. However, despite the tempting offer, Akshit had made up his mind to return to India and contribute to the growth of the Indian food industry.

When he arrived in India in 2014, Akshit was filled with excitement and a sense of purpose. He was eager to use the knowledge and skills he had acquired at AIB to help Indian businesses grow and thrive. However, he soon realized that the Indian food industry was facing many challenges, including outdated technologies, insufficient infrastructure, and a lack of proper training and education.

Despite these challenges, Akshit was determined to make a difference. He started by reaching out to local businesses and offering his services as a consultant. He used his expertise in bakery science and technology to help these businesses modernize their processes, upgrade their equipment, and improve the quality of their products.

Akshit's efforts quickly paid off, and word of his expertise began to spread. Soon, he was approached by several large food companies who were looking for his help in streamlining their operations and improving their bottom line. With his deep understanding of the industry and his commitment to helping businesses grow, Akshit was able to provide valuable insights and recommendations that led to significant improvements in efficiency and profitability.

As his reputation grew, Akshit realized that he could have an even greater impact by sharing his knowledge and expertise with a wider audience. He started conducting training sessions and workshops for food industry professionals, teaching them about the latest technologies, best practices, and proven strategies for success.

Today, Akshit is widely regarded as one of the leading experts in the Indian food industry. He has helped countless businesses grow and thrive, and he continues to inspire and educate others through his work. Despite the many challenges he faced along the way, Akshit remains steadfast in his belief that the Indian food industry has the potential to be a world leader, and he continues to work tirelessly to make that a reality.

# Understanding the Importance of Purchasing Food Ingredients

In today's competitive food industry, the importance of purchasing value-added & functional food ingredients cannot be overstated. Knowing which ingredients to buy and where to buy them from can be the difference between a delicious meal and a culinary disaster. It is important to not just buy any food ingredient, but to take into consideration the quality and freshness of the product. High quality food ingredients will not only make a dish taste better, but they will also be healthier and safer to consume. Additionally, when purchasing food ingredients, it is wise to research different sources and compare prices, as this can help to save money. Ultimately, with the right food ingredients, even the most novice of cooks can create a delicious and nourishing meal.

High-quality ingredients can enhance the flavor, aroma, and texture of food, while low-quality ingredients can negatively impact the overall experience. In addition, buying fresh and high-quality ingredients ensures food safety and reduces the risk of food borne illnesses.

Moreover, purchasing ingredients from reputable suppliers helps to ensure that the ingredients are sustainably sourced, ethically produced, and meet industry standards for quality. By investing in good ingredients, chefs and home cooks can create dishes that are not only delicious but also nourishing and safe to consume. One has to look up many factors before considering buying any ingredient.

- **Quality:** The quality of ingredients directly affects the taste, appearance, and nutritional value of the final dish. High-quality ingredients can enhance the flavor and overall experience of a meal. The quality factor is an important consideration when buying ingredients, as it can affect the taste, texture, and overall success of your dish. Some key factors to consider include:

  - **Freshness:** Choose ingredients that are as fresh as possible, especially for perishable items like fruits, vegetables, and dairy products.

  - **Flavor:** Choose ingredients that have a good flavor and aroma, as these are important for the overall taste of your dish.

- **Texture:** Look for ingredients that have the right texture for your recipe, whether it's crunchy, creamy, or tender.

- **Nutritional value:** Consider the nutritional value of ingredients, especially if you are using them in large quantities or if you have specific dietary needs.

- **Price:** Choose ingredients that are within your budget, but don't sacrifice quality for the sake of saving money.

- **Origin:** Consider the origin of ingredients, especially if you are looking for specific flavors or want to support local or sustainable agriculture.

  Remember that the quality of ingredients can greatly impact the final outcome of your dish, so it's important to choose wisely.

- **Safety:** By purchasing food ingredients from reputable and trusted sources, you can ensure that they are safe to consume and free from harmful contaminants. The safety factor is an important consideration when buying ingredients, as it affects the health and well-being of those consuming the food. Some key factors to consider include:

- **Food recalls:** Check the news and the FDA website for any recent food recalls related to the ingredients you're buying.

- **Allergen information:** Look for allergen information on the label and be aware of any potential allergens in the ingredients you are buying.

- **Packaging:** Make sure that packaging is not damaged or compromised in any way, as this can increase the risk of contamination.

- **Expiration date:** Check the expiration date of perishable ingredients, especially dairy products and meats, to ensure they are still fresh.

- **Storage conditions:** Make sure that ingredients are stored in appropriate conditions, such as refrigerated or at room temperature, to prevent spoilage and contamination.

- **Food handling:** Be mindful of how you handle food, including washing your hands and properly storing ingredients to prevent cross-contamination.

Remember that food safety is essential for maintaining good health, so be vigilant when choosing and handling ingredients.

- **Cost-effectiveness:** Proper purchasing can help control costs by ensuring that you get the best price for the ingredients you need, without sacrificing quality. To make the most cost-effective purchases when buying ingredients, consider the following:

  - **Compare prices:** Look for sales and discounts at different stores, and compare prices online to find the best deal.

  - **Buy in bulk:** Buying larger quantities can often save money in the long run, especially for items that are non-perishable and have a long shelf life.

  - **Plan meals:** Plan your meals ahead of time and make a shopping list, which will help you avoid impulse purchases and stick to what you need.

  - **Use coupons:** Look for and use coupons to reduce the cost of specific items.

  - **Buy store-brand or generic items:** Store-brand or generic items are often cheaper than their brand-name counterparts and can be just as good in quality.

  - **Shop at discount stores:** Discount stores like Aldi and Lidl can offer lower prices on groceries, as they often carry their own private label brands.

- **Grow your own:** Consider growing your own fruits and vegetables, if possible, to save on production costs.

- **Sustainability:** Choosing ingredients that are sourced responsibly, such as local and organic products, can help support the environment and promote sustainable practices. Sustainability while buying ingredients involves considering the environmental impact of the production, transportation, and disposal of the ingredients.

To make sustainable choices, you can:

1. Buy local and seasonal ingredients, which reduces the carbon footprint of transportation.

2. Choose organic ingredients, which are grown without synthetic pesticides and fertilizers, and help support sustainable agriculture.

3. Opt for ingredients that are minimally processed and packaged, to reduce waste.

4. Consider the source of ingredients, such as fair trade or products from companies with sustainable business practices.

By making conscious choices about the ingredients you buy, you can support sustainable agriculture and reduce your personal impact on the environment.

- **Flavor and diversity:** Having a variety of ingredients on hand allows for more diverse and creative meal options, leading to a more exciting and enjoyable dining experience. Flavor and diversity while buying ingredients involves choosing ingredients that not only taste great but also add variety and cultural richness to your cooking. To achieve this, you can:

    - Try new ingredients and cuisines, such as exotic spices or ingredients from different cultures.

    - Experiment with different cooking techniques, such as grilling, roasting, or baking, to bring out unique flavors in ingredients.

    - Buy ingredients from specialty stores or ethnic markets, which often carry a wider variety of items than traditional supermarkets.

    - Support local and small-scale food producers, who often use traditional methods and offer unique and high-quality ingredients.

    - By incorporating diverse ingredients and cooking methods, you can add new and exciting flavors to your meals, and explore the rich cultural heritage of food.

In conclusion, purchasing value-added food ingredients is an important consideration for any food business. These ingredients can provide a range of benefits, including, improved consistency and quality, increase shelf life of the product, and helping to get a better product and a unique selling point.

In conclusion, purchasing value-added food ingredients is an important consideration for any food business. These ingredients can provide a range of benefits, including, improved consistency and quality, increase shelf life of the product, and helping to get a better product and a unique selling point.

⬭ MORAL OF CHAPTER ⬭

The moral of the chapter is that conducting proper research into the source of food ingredients is crucial for avoiding numerous dangers in the food industry. These dangers include health risks, such as food poisoning and toxic exposure, as well as economic consequences, such as purchasing counterfeit products. In addition, not researching the source of ingredients can lead to poor quality and environmentally harmful products, as well as missed opportunities for informed decision-making and increased supply chain disruptions. It is important to research the source of ingredients in order to ensure the safety, quality, and sustainability of the food we consume.

# Chapter 1

# Importance of Researching Food Ingredient Sources

**The Dangers of Not Researching the Source of Ingredients Before Purchase**

In today's fast-paced and cost-sensitive food industry, many companies may be tempted to quickly purchase ingredients without conducting proper research into the source of those ingredients. However, this approach can lead to a range of dangerous and potentially costly consequences.

Not researching the source of food ingredients before purchasing can lead to several dangers, including:

- **Health risks:** Food ingredients from unreliable sources may be contaminated with harmful substances that can cause illness. Health risks can arise from consuming the wrong ingredients or ingredients that are not prepared or stored properly. Some common health risks include:

- **Food poisoning:** Consuming contaminated or spoiled food can cause food poisoning, which can lead to symptoms such as nausea, vomiting, diarrhea, and stomach cramps.

- **Allergic reactions:** Certain ingredients, such as nuts, dairy, or shellfish, can cause severe allergic reactions in some individuals.

- **Nutrient deficiencies:** Consuming a diet that is lacking in essential nutrients can lead to nutrient deficiencies and related health problems.

- **Toxins and pollutants:** Some ingredients, such as certain types of fish or produce grown in contaminated soil, may contain harmful toxins and pollutants.

- **Interactions with medications:** Certain ingredients, such as grapefruit or herbs, can interact with certain medications and affect their efficacy or lead to adverse side effects. It is important to be mindful of the ingredients you consume and how they are prepared and stored, to minimize health risks and ensure a balanced and healthy diet.

- **Inauthentic or counterfeit products:** Without researching the source, it can be difficult to verify the authenticity of ingredients, leading to the risk of purchasing counterfeit or inauthentic products. Counterfeit ingredients refer to ingredients that are fraudulently represented as a more expensive or premium product, or as a different ingredient altogether. This can have serious consequences, including:

    - **Health risks:** Counterfeit ingredients may contain harmful additives or contaminants, leading to potential health risks.

    - **Misleading consumers:** Counterfeit ingredients can deceive consumers into paying more for a product that is not actually what they believe they are buying.

    - **Economic impact:** Counterfeit ingredients can negatively impact the market for genuine products, and harm legitimate producers and suppliers.

    To avoid purchasing counterfeit ingredients, it is important to buy from reputable sources, such as reputable grocery stores or online retailers, and to look for authenticity seals or certifications on products. You can also research the source and history of the ingredients you are buying to ensure their authenticity.

- **Poor Quality:** Without researching the source, it's possible to purchase ingredients of poor quality, which can negatively impact the taste, appearance, and nutritional value of the final dish. Poor quality ingredients refer to ingredients that are subpar in terms of quality, freshness, or nutritional value.

  This can negatively impact the taste, texture, and overall outcome of a dish. To ensure good results, it is recommended to use fresh, high-quality ingredients that are appropriate for the intended dish.

- **Environmental harm:** By not researching the source, you may inadvertently support unsustainable practices or purchase ingredients that have been produced in ways that harm the environment.

Using certain ingredients can contribute to environmental harm. For example, ingredients sourced through environmentally damaging practices, such as unsustainable fishing methods or deforestation, can have negative impacts on ecosystems and wildlife.

Additionally, ingredients that require a large amount of energy and resources to produce, such as those grown through intensive agriculture, can contribute to greenhouse gas emissions and other environmental problems. To reduce environmental harm, it's recommended to consider the environmental impact of ingredients and choose those that have been produced in a sustainable and responsible manner.

In conclusion, failing to research the source of ingredients before a purchase can result in a range of dangerous and potentially costly consequences. From low-quality or contaminated products to non-compliant ingredients and a lack of transparency in the food supply chain, companies must take the time to thoroughly research the source of their ingredients in order to ensure the safety and quality of their products and to meet customer expectations.

Do a reality check if your vendor is well aware of the product he is selling.

Before you make any purchase decisions, it's always a good idea to do a reality check to ensure that your vendor is properly informed about the product they are offering. It is important to ask questions and make sure that they have a complete understanding of the features, benefits, and potential drawbacks of the product.

Additionally, make sure they are up-to-date on any changes or updates to the product, and that they can provide you with the most accurate information. Doing a reality check will also help you understand what kind of customer service and support you can expect from the vendor, and can help you make the best purchase decision for your needs.

Here are some steps you can take to perform a reality check on your vendor's knowledge of the product they are selling and make an informed decision:

1. **Ask specific questions about the product:** Asking the vendor detailed questions about the product and its features and functionality can give you an idea of their level of expertise. Don't be afraid to ask to follow-up questions or probe deeper into the subject.

2. **Request a demonstration:** Requesting a demonstration of the product can give you a chance to observe the product in action and ask questions about its features and functionality. This can help you understand how well the vendor knows the product.

3. It is also important to consider the shipping costs associated with any food ingredients. Excessive shipping costs can add up quickly, especially if you are purchasing in bulk. Make sure that your vendor offers competitive shipping rates to avoid any additional expenses. Additionally.

4. **Check references and reviews:** Ask the vendor for references from past customers and check online reviews of the product and the vendor. This can give you a good idea of the vendor's reputation and level of expertise. Be sure to read reviews and feedback from other customers to get a better understanding of how the product performs in real-world scenarios.

5. **Research the product yourself:** Doing your own research on the product is also a great way to verify the vendor's knowledge. Compare what they are telling you to what you read to see if they are providing accurate information.

6. Finally, consider the return policy of your vendor. Many vendors offer generous return policies, so make sure to take advantage of this in case you are not satisfied with the product.

By taking these steps, you can get a good understanding of the vendor's level of knowledge and expertise, allowing you to make an educated and informed decision about the product they are selling.

MORAL OF CHAPTER

The moral of the chapter on food safety certifications highlights the importance of verifying food safety certifications for food businesses. A food safety certification ensures compliance with regulations, boosts consumer confidence, improves business reputation, and helps with risk management. Not checking for food safety certifications can lead to contaminated food, recalls, lawsuits, and harm to the industry's reputation. In India, FSSAI certification is a legal requirement and brings many benefits to food businesses. The food industry must prioritize food safety by regularly checking certifications, implementing strong food safety systems and processes, and being transparent about their food safety practices and certifications. This is important for protecting both consumers and vulnerable populations.

# Chapter 2

# The Importance of Verifying Food Safety Certifications in the Food Industry

Compliance with food safety certifications is a critical aspect of the food industry, as it helps to ensure the safety and quality of food products. Food safety certifications are important to food products that meet certain standards for quality, safety, and hygiene and play a crucial role in protecting consumers from food borne illnesses and other health problems. Not verifying whether food suppliers have the necessary food safety certifications can be a major misstep in any food business. Without proof of certifications, it is impossible to know if the food suppliers meet the standards of safety and quality that are expected in the industry. Failing to take these steps could lead to costly consequences, such as possible food contamination and even product recalls, which can have a major impact on the reputation of the business. Therefore, it is essential for food businesses to prioritize checking for food safety certifications in order to protect their customers, as well as their own reputation.

A food safety certificate is important for several reasons:

1. **Compliance:** In many countries, obtaining a food safety certification is mandatory for food businesses to operate legally. The certification demonstrates compliance with food safety regulations and standards, which are in place to protect public health.

2. **Consumer confidence:** Having a food safety certificate can increase consumer confidence in the quality and safety of the food being sold. Consumers are more likely to purchase food products from businesses that have taken steps to ensure the safety of their products.

3. **Business reputation:** A food safety certification can enhance the reputation of a business and differentiate it from competitors who may not have taken the same precautions to ensure food safety.

4. **Risk management:** By implementing food safety measures and obtaining a certificate, food businesses can reduce the risk of food borne illness outbreaks, liability claims, and costly product recalls.

5. **Market access:** Some countries require food safety certification for businesses that want to export food products. Obtaining a certificate can open up new markets for food businesses, increasing their customer base and potential for growth.

Despite the importance of food safety certifications, many food industry players still neglect to check for them before buying food ingredients. This can result in the sale and distribution of contaminated or expired food, which can cause serious health problems and harm to consumers. In addition, it can also have serious consequences for the food industry, as it can result in recalls, lawsuits, and damage to the industry's reputation.

The Food Safety and Standards Authority of India (FSSAI) is an independent body responsible for regulating and supervising the food industry in India. Established under the Food Safety and Standards Act, 2006, FSSAI is responsible for ensuring that all food products sold in India are safe, hygienic, and of high quality.

Getting a FSSAI certificate is essential for any food business operating in India, as it demonstrates that the business is committed to food safety and quality, and that its products meet the standards set by FSSAI. A FSSAI certificate is also a legal requirement for all food businesses, as it is necessary to obtain a license from FSSAI in order to operate in the food industry.

In addition to demonstrating a commitment to food safety, having a FSSAI certificate can also bring many other benefits to a food business. For example, it can help to build consumer trust and confidence in the business, as well as enhance its reputation and credibility. It can also provide the business with access to new markets and customers, as it demonstrates that its products meet the standards required by FSSAI.

Moreover, a FSSAI certificate can also help to reduce the risk of food contamination and food borne illnesses, as it requires food businesses to implement robust food safety systems and processes. This includes adhering to strict hygiene and sanitation practices, properly storing and handling food products, and regularly monitoring food products for contamination.

To ensure compliance with food safety certifications, it is essential that food industry players adopt a proactive and vigilant approach to food safety. This includes regularly checking for food safety certifications, verifying the authenticity of certifications, and conducting regular food safety audits to ensure that food products meet the standards set by food safety certifications.

With the increasing demand for food and the globalization of food trade, ensuring the safety and quality of food products has become a major concern for governments, consumers, and food industries alike.

In addition to protecting consumers from food borne illnesses, food safety certifications also play an important role in protecting vulnerable populations. This includes young children, pregnant women, and individuals with weakened immune systems, who are at a higher risk of developing serious health problems as a result of contaminated food.

Food industry players must also ensure that they have in place robust food safety systems and processes to minimize the risk of contamination and ensure the safety of food products. This includes implementing strict hygiene and sanitation practices, properly storing and handling food products, and regularly monitoring food products for contamination.

Furthermore, food industry players must also be transparent about their food safety practices and certifications. This includes providing accurate and up-to-date information about the certifications they have received, as well as being transparent about any food safety incidents that may occur.

In conclusion, compliance with food safety certifications is a critical aspect of the food industry. Food industry players must be proactive and vigilant in ensuring the safety and quality of food products and must adopt robust food safety systems and processes to minimize the risk of contamination. In addition, they must be transparent about their food safety practices and certifications and be committed to protecting the health and well-being of consumers. Failure to comply with food safety certifications can result in serious consequences for both consumers and the food industry and must be taken seriously by all players in the food industry.

The moral of the chapter on "The Significance of Contracts in the F&B industry" could be summarized as follows:

- **Contracts are crucial in the F&B industry:** Contracts are an essential tool for establishing agreements and defining the obligations and responsibilities of all parties involved in the F&B industry.

- **Timing is key:** In the F&B industry, timing is critical, and contracts should be in place well in advance of any critical dates, such as the start of a new season or the launch of a new product.

- **Key considerations:** When forming contracts in the F&B industry, it is important to consider factors such as product quality, delivery schedules, and payment terms.

- **How long to contract for:** The length of a contract in the F&B industry can vary depending on the specific needs and circumstances of the parties involved. However, contracts should be structured to provide stability and certainty while also allowing for flexibility and adaptation to changing circumstances.

Chapter 3

# Safeguarding your Interests: The Significance of Contracts

## The Significance of Contracts

Not making a contract can be a risky move for any business. Without an agreement in place, there is no guarantee that the terms of any agreement will be honored and fulfilled. Furthermore, it can be difficult to prove who is at fault if something goes wrong, and there is no written document to refer to as a source of evidence. Without a contract, there is no protection for either party and any dispute could result in costly and lengthy legal proceedings.

Consequently, it is always advisable to make a contract, clearly outlining the responsibilities and expectations of both parties. Doing so will provide a level of assurance that both parties are aware of their obligations and that these will be adhered to. A contract should be written in plain language and be easy to understand so that both parties are aware of their rights and obligations. It is also important to ensure that the food ingredients you purchase are of high quality. Poor quality ingredients can have a negative impact on the taste and texture of the food you are cooking, and can also leave a bad impression on your customers. To avoid such a situation, it is important to research the suppliers you are considering and make sure that the ingredients they provide are of good quality.

Additionally, it is important to read reviews and speak to other customers who have purchased food ingredients from the supplier in the past. This will give you a better indication of the quality of the ingredients and the reliability of the supplier. Finally, it is important to check the expiration dates of the food ingredients you are purchasing, to ensure that they are still safe to eat.

Essential Guide to Agreements, Purchase Orders and Contracts in Procurement

## What is an agreement?

A sales contract agreement is a legally binding document that outlines the terms and conditions of a sale transaction between a buyer and a seller. It specifies the details of the goods or services being sold, including the price, payment terms, delivery schedule, and any warranties or guarantees. The sales contract agreement protects both the buyer and the seller by clearly defining the terms and conditions of the sale, reducing the risk of misunderstandings or disputes.

The sales contract agreement may also include provisions for dispute resolution, such as mediation or arbitration, and specify the law that will govern the agreement. It is important to carefully review and understand the terms and conditions of the sales contract agreement before signing it, as it creates a legally binding obligation for both parties to fulfill the terms outlined in the agreement.

## What is a Purchase Order

A purchase order (PO) is a document that is issued by a buyer to a supplier, which outlines the details of a specific order for goods or services. The following are the key elements that should be included in a purchase order issued to a supplier:

- **Purchase Order Number:** A unique identification number should be assigned to each purchase order to ensure accurate tracking and referencing.

- **Date:** The date the purchase order was issued should be clearly stated.

- **Supplier Information:** The supplier's name, address, and contact information should be clearly stated.

- **Buyer Information:** The buyer's name, address, and contact information should be clearly stated.

- **Product or Service Details:** The product or service being purchased should be described in detail, including specifications, quantity, and unit price.

- **Delivery Information:** The delivery date, delivery address, and any special delivery requirements should be stated.

- **Payment Terms:** The payment terms, including the method of payment, payment due date, and any discounts or promotions, should be stated.

- **Warranty Information:** Any warranty information related to the product or service should be stated.

- **Acceptance and Approval:** A signature line should be included for the supplier to sign, indicating their acceptance and agreement to the terms outlined in the purchase order.

- **Terms and Conditions:** Any additional terms and conditions should be stated, such as return policies, cancellation policies, and dispute resolution processes.

It is important to ensure that the purchase order accurately reflects the terms and conditions of the agreement between the buyer and the supplier. By including all relevant information in the purchase order, the buyer can ensure that the transaction runs smoothly and that all parties have a clear understanding of the terms and conditions of the agreement.

Verifying a purchase order with a sales contract is important for several reasons:

- **Ensures Accuracy:** Verifying a purchase order with a sales contract ensures that the terms and conditions of the sale, as outlined in the sales contract, are accurately reflected in the purchase order. This helps to prevent misunderstandings or disputes between the buyer and the seller.

- **Reduces Risk:** By verifying that the purchase order accurately reflects the terms and conditions of the sales contract, both the buyer and the seller can reduce the risk of disputes or legal issues arising from the transaction.

- **Protects Interests:** Verifying a purchase order with a sales contract helps to protect the interests of both the buyer and the seller. The buyer can ensure that they receive the goods or services as outlined in the sales contract, while the seller can be sure that they are paid the agreed-upon price for the goods or services they provide.

- **Increases Confidence:** Verifying a purchase order with a sales contract increases confidence in the transaction and helps to build trust between the buyer and the seller.

It is recommended that both the buyer and the seller carefully review and verify the purchase order and the sales contract before signing them, to ensure that all the terms and conditions of the sale are accurately reflected and agreed upon by both parties. This helps to minimize the risk of misunderstandings or disputes and ensures that the transaction runs smoothly.

## The Importance of Signing a Contract Copy and Issuing a Purchase Order at the Time of Purchase.

It is essential to ensure that all parties involved in a transaction are aware of the terms and conditions of the agreement. By signing a contract copy and issuing a purchase order, both the buyer and seller are fully informed of the terms of the purchase, including any warranties, guarantees, and delivery dates. This will ensure that the transaction is conducted with full knowledge and understanding on both sides and that any disputes that arise can be quickly and fairly resolved.

Moreover, the contract copy provides a legal document that can be referred to in the future, in the event of any disagreements. Furthermore, a purchase order is also critical for accounting purposes, as it helps to track all financial transactions related to the purchase. In this way, it serves to protect both the buyer and the seller, and helps to ensure that the transaction is conducted in a professional and efficient manner.

In any business transaction, it is essential to have a clear understanding of the terms and conditions of the agreement between the buyer and the seller. One of the most effective ways to ensure that everyone is on the same page is by signing a contract copy and issuing a purchase order at the time of purchase. In this article, we will discuss the importance of these two documents in ensuring that the transaction runs smoothly.

1.  **Legal Protection:** A contract copy is a legally binding document that outlines the terms and conditions of the agreement between the buyer and the seller. By signing a contract copy, both parties agree to abide by the terms and conditions outlined in the document, which provides legal protection in the event of any disputes.

2.  **Clarity of Terms:** A contract copy provides clarity on the terms and conditions of the agreement, including the price, payment terms, delivery schedule, and any other important details. This helps to ensure that both parties have a clear understanding of the agreement, which can help to prevent misunderstandings and disputes.

3. **Purchase Order:** A purchase order is a document that confirms the details of the transaction, including the price, payment terms, delivery schedule, and any other important details. By issuing a purchase order at the time of purchase, the buyer can ensure that the transaction is recorded and that all parties have a clear understanding of the terms and conditions of the agreement.

4. **Record Keeping:** A purchase order serves as an official record of the transaction and can be used for record-keeping purposes, such as tracking deliveries, reconciling payments, and monitoring budgets. This helps to ensure that the transaction runs smoothly and that all parties have a clear understanding of the terms and conditions of the agreement.

5. **Improved Communication:** By signing a contract copy and issuing a purchase order at the time of purchase, the buyer and the seller have a clear understanding of the terms and conditions of the agreement, which can improve communication and help to resolve any issues that may arise during the transaction.

In conclusion, signing a contract copy and issuing a purchase order at the time of purchase are essential steps in ensuring that the transaction runs smoothly.

These documents provide legal protection, clarity of terms, serve as an official record of the transaction and can improve communication between the buyer and the seller. By taking these steps, the buyer can ensure that the transaction is recorded and that all parties have a clear understanding of the terms and conditions of the agreement, which can help to prevent misunderstandings and disputes.

**Timing is Key: Strategies for Successful Contracting**

To contract at the right time, it is important to consider the following factors:

1. **Market conditions:** Consider the current state of the market and the conditions that might affect the contract. Market conditions are the economic, financial, and industry-specific factors that can affect the demand for and supply of goods and services. Market conditions play a crucial role in determining the terms of a contract, including the price, quantity, and delivery terms.

   - **Economic conditions:** Economic conditions such as inflation, unemployment, and consumer confidence can affect demand for goods and services, and in turn, influence the terms of a contract.

- **Financial conditions:** Financial conditions such as interest rates, credit availability, and currency exchange rates can also affect demand and supply, and thus, impact the terms of a contract.

- **Industry-specific conditions:** Industry-specific conditions such as competition, regulatory environment, and technological advancements can also influence the terms of a contract.

- **Supply and demand dynamics:** The balance of supply and demand in a market can also impact the terms of a contract, as businesses will be more likely to agree to favorable terms when demand is high and supply is limited.

- When entering into a contract, it is important for businesses to consider the current and expected market conditions, as these can have a significant impact on the terms of the agreement. A thorough understanding of market conditions can help businesses negotiate favorable terms and manage their risks effectively.

2. **Timing:** Identify the best time to sign the contract based on the project timeline, availability of resources, and other relevant factors. The timing of a contract can have a significant impact on its success and outcome. Some factors to consider when timing a contract include:

   - **Market conditions:** Timing a contract during favorable market conditions, such as high demand and low supply, can result in more favorable terms for the parties involved.

   - **Capacity:** The timing of a contract should take into account the parties' capacity to fulfill their obligations, such as available resources, manpower, and production capacity.

   - **Lead time:** The lead time required to deliver goods or services should be considered when timing a contract. A contract that requires a quick turnaround time may need to be entered into at an earlier stage to allow enough time for preparation and delivery.

   - **Seasonal trends:** Some industries have seasonal trends that affect demand, and the timing of a contract should take these trends into account. For example, a contract for holiday decorations should be entered into well in advance of the holiday season.

- **Legal requirements:** The timing of a contract should also take into account any legal requirements, such as registration, filing, and compliance with regulations.

3. **Negotiations:** Negotiate the terms and conditions of the contract to ensure that they are favorable to both parties.

Contract negotiation is the process of reaching an agreement on the terms of a contract between two or more parties. Negotiating a contract involves several steps, including:

- **Preparation:** Before entering into negotiations, both parties should prepare by gathering information, researching market conditions, and setting goals and objectives.

- **Identifying key terms:** The parties should identify the key terms of the contract, such as price, delivery terms, and warranties, that they want to negotiate.

- **Exploring each other's positions:** During negotiations, the parties should listen to each other's positions and interests, and try to understand their motivations and concerns.

- **Brainstorming and compromising:** Both parties should engage in brainstorming and compromising to identify creative solutions that meet the needs of both sides.

- **Drafting the agreement:** Once an agreement has been reached, the terms should be drafted into a legally binding contract.

- **Review and finalization:** The contract should be reviewed by both parties to ensure that it accurately reflects the terms of the agreement and is legally binding.

    Effective contract negotiation requires good communication, collaboration, and a willingness to compromise. By engaging in a fair and transparent negotiation process, both parties can reach an agreement that is mutually beneficial and reduces the risk of disputes in the future.

4. **Due diligence:** Carefully review the contract and assess any potential risks before signing it. Due diligence is the process of carefully evaluating a potential investment or business opportunity to assess its risks and potential rewards. In the context of contract making, due diligence refers

to the steps taken to ensure that both parties have a clear understanding of the terms and conditions of the contract before it is signed.

Here are some key steps to consider when conducting due diligence during the contract-making process:

- **Review the terms and conditions:** Carefully review the terms and conditions of the contract, including the scope of work, payment terms, deadlines, and any other relevant details.

- **Verify the parties involved:** Ensure that all parties involved in the contract have the authority to enter into the agreement and are properly identified.

- **Evaluate the financial stability of the parties:** Assess the financial stability of the parties involved in the contract, including their creditworthiness and ability to fulfill their obligations under the contract.

- **Review any legal or regulatory requirements:** Ensure that the contract complies with any applicable laws and regulations, including labor laws, tax laws, and environmental regulations.

- **Verify insurance coverage:** Ensure that all parties involved in the contract have adequate insurance coverage to protect against potential risks.

- **Obtain independent expert advice:** If necessary, obtain independent expert advice, such as legal or financial advice, to ensure that the terms and conditions of the contract are fully understood and properly evaluated.

- **Negotiate any necessary changes:** If necessary, negotiate any changes to the contract to ensure that all parties are fully satisfied with the terms and conditions of the agreement.

  Conducting due diligence during the contract-making process is essential to ensure that both parties fully understand the terms and conditions of the agreement and to minimize potential risks and liabilities. By following these steps, you can ensure that your contract is properly evaluated and that both parties are fully protected.

5. **Legal advice:** Seek legal advice from a qualified attorney to ensure that the contract is legally binding and enforceable. Seeking legal advice

while making a contract is important to ensure that the contract is legally binding, enforceable, and complies with all relevant laws and regulations. Legal advice can also help to identify and mitigate any potential risks or liabilities associated with the contract.

Here are some key reasons why seeking legal advice while making a contract is important:

- **Understanding the legal requirements:** A legal professional can help you understand the legal requirements for entering into a contract, including any applicable laws and regulations.

- **Reviewing the contract terms:** Legal advice can help to review the terms and conditions of the contract to ensure that they are clear, accurate, and enforceable.

- **Identifying potential risks and liabilities:** Legal advice can help to identify any potential risks or liabilities associated with the contract and to develop strategies to mitigate these risks.

- **Negotiating changes to the contract:** Legal advice can help to negotiate any necessary changes to the contract to ensure that both parties are fully satisfied with the terms and conditions of the agreement.

- **Protecting your rights and interests:** Legal advice can help to protect your rights and interests by ensuring that the contract is legally binding and enforceable.

- **Minimizing the risk of disputes:** Legal advice can help to minimize the risk of disputes by ensuring that the contract is clear and unambiguous and that both parties have a clear understanding of their obligations and responsibilities.

In conclusion, seeking legal advice while making a contract is an important step to ensure that the contract is legally binding, and enforceable, and protects the rights and interests of both parties. By working with a legal professional, you can ensure that your contract is properly evaluated and that all necessary steps are taken to minimize potential risks and liabilities.

By taking these factors into consideration, you can contract at the right time and ensure that your agreements are successful and beneficial for all parties involved.

**Key Considerations in Contract Formation Covid**

The consideration of a contract should include the purpose of the contract, the parties involved, the obligations of the contracting parties, the terms of the agreement, the consideration exchanged, the duration of the contract, and any other relevant information.

It is important to note that contracts are legally binding, so all parties should read and understand the contract before signing. Additionally, all parties should include any additional terms and conditions they wish to incorporate into the contract.

Furthermore, any modifications to the agreement should be made in writing to ensure that all parties are in agreement with the changes. Lastly, all parties should review the finalized contract to ensure that it accurately reflects their intentions and expectations. Taking time to thoroughly consider each of these elements will help to ensure that all parties are protected and that the contract terms are respected.

There are various factors that has to be considered in contract formation:

## Pandemic

The COVID-19 pandemic has had a significant impact on contracts. Due to the lockdowns, business closures, and supply chain disruptions caused by the pandemic, many contracts have been disrupted or terminated.

In some cases, parties to the contract have invoked "force majeure" clauses to excuse their performance due to unforeseen circumstances. Additionally, disputes have arisen over issues such as price increases, delays in delivery, and non-delivery of goods and services.

To mitigate the impact of the pandemic on contracts, it is recommended to review and update force majeure clauses, establish clear communication with all parties, and seek legal advice where necessary. During the COVID-19 pandemic, the timing for contracting may be impacted by a number of factors.

These could include:

- **Supply chain disruptions:** Many industries have faced supply chain disruptions due to the pandemic, which can impact the availability of goods and services.

- **Remote work:** The shift to remote work has affected the timing and execution of contracts, as many companies have had to adjust to new ways of working.

- **Economic uncertainty:** The pandemic has led to economic uncertainty, which may impact the timing of contracts as companies assess their financial stability and resources.

- **Government policies:** Government policies related to the pandemic, such as lockdowns and restrictions on business operations, may impact the timing of contracts.

- It is important to carefully consider these factors and communicate effectively with all parties involved when contracting during the COVID-19 pandemic.

## Shipping Delay

If a shipping delay is affecting a contract, it may be considered a breach of contract if the delay causes one of the parties to not fulfill their obligations as specified in the agreement. The affected party may be entitled to compensation or other remedies, such as termination of the contract if the delay is significant.

It's best to review the specific terms of the contract and consult a lawyer to understand the rights and obligations of both parties in this situation.

Shipping delays can impact the timing of contracts and may result in missed deadlines and additional costs. To minimize the impact of shipping delays, it is important to consider the following strategies:

- **Plan ahead:** Anticipate potential shipping delays and build extra time into your schedule to accommodate them.

- **Choose reliable carriers:** Select carriers that have a track record of delivering goods on time and provide up-to-date tracking information.

- **Use real-time tracking:** Use real-time tracking tools to monitor the status of shipments and receive updates on any delays.

- **Communicate with suppliers:** Regularly communicate with suppliers to understand any potential shipping delays and take proactive measures to minimize their impact.

- **Consider alternative shipping options:** If a shipment is delayed, consider alternative shipping options, such as expedited delivery or air freight, to minimize the impact on your schedule.

## Custom

Custom duties, also known as tariffs, can impact contracts in several ways. They can increase the cost of goods or services being imported, making them more expensive for the importing party, potentially causing the terms of the contract to be renegotiated. Custom duties can also lead to delays in the delivery of goods or services, disrupting the timeline outlined in the contract.

In some cases, custom duties may make it uneconomical for a party to fulfill their obligations under the contract, potentially leading to a breach of contract. To minimize the impact of custom duties on contracts, it is important for both parties to consider and include provisions for tariffs in their agreements.

Custom duty is a tax imposed by a government on imported goods. It is based on the value of the goods and their classification under the Harmonized system of tariffs. Custom duties are collected at the point of entry into a country and are used to protect domestic industries, generate revenue, and regulate trade.

When contracting for the import of goods, it is important to consider the potential impact of custom duties on the cost of the goods and the delivery timeline. To minimize the impact of custom duties:

- **Review customs regulations**

  Familiarize yourself with the customs regulations and procedures in the importing country, including the classification of the goods and the applicable duty rates.

- **Negotiate with suppliers**

  Consider negotiating with suppliers to include the cost of custom duties in the price of the goods or to split the cost between the parties.

- **Utilize duty-free provisions**

  If available, utilize duty-free provisions or trade agreements to minimize the impact of custom duties on the cost of the goods.

- **Plan for payment**

  Ensure that adequate funds are available to pay for custom duties and that the payment process is well-coordinated.

## Local transport

Local transportation disruptions can have an impact on contracts, especially if the contract requires goods or services to be delivered by a specific date and location.

The aim of local transportation is to provide convenient and affordable mobility options for people to move within the area. The options available vary depending on the location and infrastructure.

Delays in transportation can cause disruptions in the supply chain and result in failure to meet the contract terms, leading to penalties or termination of the contract. In such cases, it's important to have clear clauses in the contract addressing the potential impact of transportation disruptions, such as provisions for extensions of delivery time or alternative delivery methods.

## Weather

Weather can have a significant impact on contracts, especially in industries such as construction, agriculture, and transportation. Weather conditions can cause delays, increase costs, and make it difficult to perform contractual obligations.

In transportation contracts, severe weather can make it difficult or impossible to fulfill the obligations under the contract, leading to potential disputes over force majeure or frustration of purpose.

In some contracts, there may be specific provisions regarding weather-related issues such as "force majeure" clauses, which excuse performance in the event of unforeseen circumstances, including severe weather. However, in the absence of such provisions, parties may still be able to claim relief from their obligations based on the common law doctrine of "frustration" if weather makes performance impossible or radically different from what was originally agreed.

It's important for parties to consider the potential impact of weather on their contract and to include provisions to address these issues in order to minimize the risk of disputes.

In general, it is recommended to include clear and detailed provisions in contracts that address the potential impact of weather, such as specifying how delays or cancellations will be handled, and which party will bear the risk of weather-related losses.

**How long should you contract for?**

When it comes to signing a contract, it is important to consider how long it should be for. There are a few factors to consider when deciding on the length of the contract, such as the purpose of the agreement, the scope of the work to be completed, the timeline for project completion, and any potential risks associated with the contract. It is also important to consider if either party wants to be able to review and renew or renegotiate the contract at certain points. In general, if you are unclear about the length of a contract, it is best to err on the side of caution and make the contract for a longer period of time, as it is typically easier to shorten the agreement in the future if necessary than it is to extend it.

Some common factors that influence the length of a contract include the duration of the project or services being provided, the level of commitment required from each party, and any legal or regulatory requirements that may apply.

For example, employment contracts may last for a fixed period of time, such as one year, or they may be open-ended with a probationary period. Renting a property may require a lease agreement for a specific number of months or years. Service agreements with a consultant or contractor may be for a defined project or on a retainer basis.

In general, the length of a contract should be appropriate for the specific situation and provide sufficient time for both parties to fulfill their obligations. It's important to carefully review and understand the terms of the agreement before signing it to ensure that it meets your needs and expectations.

The length of a contract can vary depending on the type of agreement and the terms being agreed upon. Some common contract lengths include:

- **Short-term contracts**

  These contracts typically last for a period of less than a year and are often used for temporary projects or short-term engagements.

- **Medium-term contracts**

  These contracts can last anywhere from one to three years and are often used for more complex projects or ongoing engagements that require a longer commitment.

- **Long-term contracts**

  These contracts can last for several years, even up to a decade or more, and are often used for strategic partnerships, major projects, or significant investments.

The length of a contract should reflect the nature and duration of the relationship being established. It is important to carefully consider the terms and conditions of a contract, including the length, before signing it.

⬭ MORAL OF CHAPTER ⬭

---

The Moral of Chapter is that L1, L2, and L3 purchase pricing strategy can be a useful tool for procurement, but it's important to understand its limitations and be aware of the potential problems that can arise. By taking a personalized approach and carefully evaluating each supplier and their products, businesses can reap the benefits of this strategy while avoiding its potential pitfalls.

Chapter 4

# Understanding and Implementing Effective Bidding Purchase Pricing Techniques

**L1, L2, and L3 Purchase Pricing Strategy: Understanding its Benefits and Limitations**

In procurement, it's essential to have a clear and effective strategy for purchasing goods and services. One such strategy is the L1, L2, and L3 purchase pricing strategy, also known as bidding strategies, which categorizes suppliers based on their level of competitiveness and potential for providing the best value for money.

L1 represents the most competitive and preferred supplier, L2 represents the secondary supplier, and L3 represents the least competitive supplier.

While the L1, L2, and L3 purchase pricing strategy may seem like a straightforward solution to procurement, it's essential to consider whether it is truly working in your business. The success of this strategy depends on several factors, including the quality of suppliers, the ability to negotiate favorable terms, and the ability to manage risk.

One potential problem with this strategy is that it can be difficult to determine the most competitive supplier. A supplier may appear competitive based on price, but their quality may be subpar, resulting in additional costs in the long term. Additionally, relying too heavily on one supplier can create a significant risk for a business if the supplier is unable to deliver goods or services as expected.

One of the major problems with the L1, L2, and L3 purchase pricing strategy is that the buyer might end up purchasing a duplicate or substandard product. When suppliers are categorized based on their competitiveness, it's possible that a supplier may compromise on quality to offer a lower price. This can result in the buyer receiving a product that is not fit for its intended purpose, leading to additional costs in terms of time and resources to replace the product.

Another problem is that suppliers may not provide accurate information about their products, leading to unexpected costs. For example, a supplier may provide a low quote for a product, but the actual cost may be significantly higher due to hidden fees or additional charges.

It's important for buyers to consider these potential problems when implementing the L1, L2, and L3 purchase pricing strategy. By being aware of these limitations, buyers can take steps to mitigate these risks and ensure that they receive high-quality products at the best possible price.

Despite these potential problems, there are several advantages to using the L1, L2, and L3 purchase pricing strategy. By categorizing suppliers based on their competitiveness, a business can negotiate more favorable terms and reduce the overall cost of procurement. Additionally, by having multiple suppliers, a business can mitigate the risk associated with relying too heavily on one supplier.

**Example**

I would like to explain this with an example. Once upon a time, there was a small bakery located in the heart of the city "Delhi". The owner, Mr. Aggarwal, had been running the business for over ten years and was known for his delicious baked goods. Mr. Aggarwal was always looking for ways to improve her business, so when he heard about the L1, L2, and L3 purchase pricing strategy, he was eager to try it.

The strategy involved categorizing suppliers based on their competitiveness and prioritizing the most competitive suppliers for future purchases. Mr.

Aggarwal thought this would be a great way to save money on ingredients and improve his margins.

However, things didn't go as planned. He started purchasing his flour from a new supplier who offered the lowest quote among his L1 suppliers. The flour was significantly cheaper than what he had been using, but it also had a lower quality. As a result, his baked goods didn't turn out as well as they had before and customers started complaining.

Mr. Aggarwal quickly realized his mistake and switched back to his original supplier, but the damage had already been done. His reputation had taken a hit and he was now facing significant losses.

Mr. Aggarwal learned a valuable lesson about the importance of considering not only the price, but also the quality of ingredients. He realized that the L1, L2, and L3 purchase pricing strategy was not a one-size-fits-all solution and that he needed to take a more personalized approach to purchasing.

From that day on, he made sure to carefully evaluate each supplier and their products before making a purchase. He was able to find the right balance between price and quality, and his bakery was once again thriving.

In conclusion, the L1, L2, and L3 purchase pricing strategy can be a useful tool for procurement. However, it's essential to consider the limitations and potential problems associated with this strategy and ensure it is aligned with the overall goals of the business.

The Moral of Chapter is that the cost of ingredients plays a crucial role in the profitability of a business. By keeping a close eye on the expenses, including the dosage and percentage cost of ingredients, a business can achieve substantial savings in the long term. By switching to a better ingredient, a business can reduce the overall cost of production and increase its profitability. It is important to consider both the dosage and the percentage cost of ingredients when making decisions about which ingredients to use in production. By being mindful of these costs, a business can ensure long-term sustainability and continued success.

# Chapter 5

# Money Maths: The Hidden Costs of High Dosages

As a business owner, it's important to keep a close eye on the expenses and make sure you're not overspending on ingredients. One common issue that many businesses face is using high dosages of ingredients, which can add up over time and significantly impact your bottom line. In this chapter, we'll explore the consequences of high dosage, and provide tips for maximizing your savings.

**The Cost of High Dosage**

When it comes to ingredients, the amount used can have a huge impact on your expenses. For example, you're using an ingredient that costs ₹1,000 per kilogram and in a batch size of 100kg, you're using 5kg of this ingredient. The cost of using 5kg of the ingredient in a batch size of 100kg is ₹5,000.

Now, let's consider switching to a better functional ingredient that costs ₹1,100 per kilogram. By switching to this better ingredient, you can reduce the dosage by

15%. This means that instead of using 5kg of the original ingredient, you would now use 4.25kg of the better ingredient.

The cost of using 4.25kg of the better ingredient in a batch size of 100kg would be ₹4,675.

Comparing the cost of using 5kg of the original ingredient with the cost of using 4.25kg of the better ingredient, you would save ₹5,000 - ₹4,675 = ₹325 per 100kg batch size. In other words, switching to the better ingredient would result in a saving of ₹3.25 per kilogram.

Let's continue with the scenario where the business is using 4.25kg of the better functional ingredient in a batch size of 100kg, and produces 1000MT (1000 x 1000kg) of the product each month.

The cost of using 4.25kg of the better ingredient in a batch size of 100kg is ₹4,675. So, the cost of producing 100kg of the product with the better ingredient is ₹4,675. And, the cost of producing 1000MT (1000 x 100kg) of the product each month would be ₹4,675 x 1000 = ₹4,675,000.

If the business was still using the original ingredient at a cost of ₹5,000 per 100kg, the cost of producing 1000MT of the product each month would be ₹5,000 x 1000 = ₹5,000,000.

Comparing these two costs, the business would save ₹5,000,000 - ₹4,675,000 = ₹325,000 each month by switching to the better ingredient.

On an annual basis, the business would save ₹325,000 x 12 = ₹3,900,000. So, in a year, the business would save ₹3,900,000 by switching to the better functional ingredient.

This shows the significance of considering the cost of ingredients when it comes to running a business. By taking the time to adjust your receipts and consider the cost of ingredients, you can achieve substantial savings in the long term.

**To Sum Up**

**The first ingredient,** "Cheaper Ingredient," has a price of ₹1,000 per kilogram and is used in a dose of 5 kilograms per 100 kilograms batch, resulting in a cost of ₹5,000 for the ingredient in a 100 kilograms batch. In a 1000 metric tons batch, the cost of the ingredient would be ₹5,000,000.

**The second ingredient,** "Premium Ingredients," has a price of ₹1,100 per kilogram and is used in a dose of 4.25 kilograms per 100 kilograms batch, resulting in a cost of ₹4,675 for the ingredient in a 100 kilograms batch. In a 1000 metric tons batch, the cost of the ingredient would be ₹4,675,000.

The table also calculates the savings per 100 kilograms batch and per 1000 metric tons batch. Using the premium ingredient instead of the cheaper ingredient results in a savings of ₹325 per 100 kilograms batch and ₹325,000 per 1000 metric tons batch. The **annual savings** by using the premium ingredient instead of the cheaper ingredient is calculated to be ₹3,900,000.

## The Importance of Checking Percentage Cost in Ingredients.

When running a business, it is essential to be mindful of the costs associated with production. One of the most significant costs is the cost of ingredients. While it may seem like a small detail, the cost of ingredients can add up quickly and significantly impact the overall profitability of a business. That's why it's crucial to not only check the dosage of ingredients, but also the percentage cost of that ingredient.

By reducing the percentage cost of an ingredient by just 1%, a business can result in savings of 6-7% in higher margins. This is because the cost of ingredients usually makes up a significant portion of the overall cost of production. When a business reduces the cost of ingredients, it also reduces the overall cost of production, leading to increased profitability.

Switching to a better ingredient can achieve two goals in one shot. Firstly, by reducing the dosage of the ingredient, a business reduces the overall cost of production. Secondly, by switching to a better ingredient, a business also reduces the percentage cost of the ingredient, resulting in further savings. The result is a significant saving per kilogram of product.

Here's an example table that demonstrates the importance of checking the percentage cost of ingredients in Indian Rupees (INR):

The purpose of this table is to show the importance of checking the percentage cost of each ingredient in a recipe.

Each ingredient is listed in a separate row and consists of four columns: Ingredient, Quantity, Cost (INR), and Percentage Cost. The Ingredient column lists the names of the ingredients used in the recipe, the Quantity column lists the amount of each ingredient used, the Cost (INR) column lists the cost of each ingredient in Indian Rupees, and the Percentage Cost column lists the percentage of the total cost that each ingredient represents.

In this example, the cost of flour is 70 INR for 1 kg and it represents 7% of the total cost. The cost of sugar is 20 INR for 500 g and it represents 2.5% of the total cost. The cost of salt is 5 INR for 50 g and it represents 10% of the total cost.

By checking the percentage cost of each ingredient, it becomes easier to determine which ingredients are more expensive and which ones are less expensive in comparison to the others. This information can be useful in adjusting the recipe to reduce costs or improve the quality of the final product.

To Sum Up, money maths is an important aspect of running a successful business. By being mindful of the cost of high dosages and considering alternative functional ingredients, you can maximize your savings and improve your bottom line. Don't hesitate to take a closer look at your receipts and make changes where necessary – small adjustments can lead to big savings in the long run.

⬭ MORAL OF CHAPTER ⬭

---

The moral of the chapter on cost-quality trade-off is that businesses must strike a balance between the cost of a product or service and its quality. Ignoring this relationship can lead to negative consequences for the business, such as decreased customer satisfaction and harm to the company's reputation. It is important for businesses to consider factors such as the target market, production process, and cost-saving technologies when making decisions about the cost-quality trade-off. This can help to ensure that the business is getting the best value for its money and achieving its goals. Continuous evaluation and adjustment of the cost-quality trade-off is crucial to remain competitive in the market and maintain a strong brand image. Ultimately, balancing the cost-quality trade-off is a critical aspect of decision making for businesses.

Chapter 6

# Value Engineered Offering

**Ignoring the Cost-Quality Trade-Off**

The cost-quality trade-off refers to the relationship between the cost of a product or service and its quality. In general, the higher the quality, the higher the cost. Conversely, the lower the quality, the lower the cost. This trade-off is a common challenge for businesses, as they must balance the need to keep costs low with the need to provide high-quality products to meet customer demands and remain competitive.

Ignoring the cost-quality trade-off can be a mistake when making decisions regarding a business or a project. This is because, in many cases, the cost of a product or service will have an impact on its quality, and vice versa. For example, if you are looking to purchase a piece of furniture or an appliance, you may find that the cheaper models will not be as durable or well-built as the more expensive models. On the other hand, if you are looking to hire a contractor or a professional service provider, the lower-cost options may not have the same level of skill or experience.

Therefore, it is crucial to take into account the cost-quality trade-off when making decisions. This can help to ensure that you are getting the best value for your money and achieving your goals. To do this, businesses must consider several factors, including the target market, the production process, and the use of cost-saving technologies. Ultimately, the decision on the cost-quality trade-off depends on the goals and objectives of the business, as well as the needs and expectations of its target market.

Additionally, it is important for businesses to continuously evaluate and adjust the cost-quality trade-off as market conditions and customer demands change. A business that offers high-quality products at a premium price may find that it is not sustainable in a market where customers are price-sensitive. On the other hand, a business that focuses solely on cutting costs may find that it is unable to compete with competitors offering higher quality products.

The cost-quality trade-off can also have an impact on a company's reputation and brand image. Poor quality products, regardless of their low cost, can harm a company's reputation and negatively impact customer loyalty. On the other hand, high-quality products that are priced affordably can help to build a strong brand and increase customer loyalty.

**Example**

Once upon a time, there was a small bakery in a small town. The bakery was well-known for its delicious cakes and pastries. The owner, Mrs. Baker, was proud of her bakery and was determined to provide the best quality products to her customers. She always used the finest ingredients and took great care to make each cake and pastry by hand. However, as the popularity of the bakery grew, Mrs. Baker realized that she was facing a problem. Her costs were increasing, and she was having a difficult time keeping up with demand.

One day, Mrs. Baker heard about a new ingredient that was much cheaper than the one she was using. She thought that using this ingredient would help her reduce costs and keep up with demand. However, when she tried it out, she realized that the cakes and pastries were not as delicious as they used to be. The customers noticed the difference, and many of them started to choose other bakeries.

Mrs. Baker soon realized that she had made a mistake. She had ignored the cost-quality trade-off and focused only on cutting costs. She realized that the quality of her products was what made her bakery unique, and she couldn't afford to compromise on that.

Mrs. Baker decided to switch back to her original ingredients, even though they were more expensive.

She knew that this would increase her costs, but she also knew that it was the right thing to do. She was willing to pay the extra cost to ensure that her customers continued to enjoy the high-quality cakes and pastries they had come to expect.

The customers noticed the improvement in quality, and the bakery's popularity began to grow again. Mrs. Baker learned an important lesson about the importance of balancing the cost-quality trade-off. She understood that cutting costs was important, but not at the expense of quality. By taking a balanced approach, she was able to provide her customers with high-quality products, maintain her reputation, and grow her business.

In the end, Mrs. Baker learned that the cost-quality trade-off is a delicate balance and that businesses must be mindful of this relationship when making decisions. By considering the target market, production process, and cost-saving technologies, businesses can make informed decisions that help them achieve their goals while also meeting customer demands.

In conclusion, balancing the cost-quality trade-off is a critical aspect of decision-making for businesses. It is important to consider the needs and expectations of the target market, the production process, and the use of cost-saving technologies to make informed decisions that help to achieve business goals while also meeting customer demands. By continuously evaluating and adjusting the cost-quality trade-off, businesses can remain competitive and maintain a strong brand image in the market. Food industry player must take a proactive and vigilant approach to these factors, investing in the knowledge and resources needed to ensure that they are making informed purchasing decisions, and taking into account all factors that may affect the cost and quantity of the ingredients being purchased. Failure to compare prices and quantities can result in serious consequences for the food industry and must be avoided at all costs.

MORAL OF CHAPTER

---

The food industry is responsible for ensuring that the food ingredients it sells and distributes are safe, fresh, and of high quality. To achieve this, it is crucial for food industry players to properly evaluate packaging and storage requirements, as neglecting this step can have serious consequences for product quality, food safety, cost-effectiveness, and legal compliance.

Product quality can be impacted if packaging and storage requirements are not evaluated, as it can lead to product damage during transportation or storage, reducing customer satisfaction. Food safety can also be jeopardized if specific packaging and storage conditions are not met, as this can allow the growth of harmful bacteria and microorganisms that can cause food borne illness.

Also, neglecting to evaluate packaging and storage requirements can result in increased costs for businesses due to product waste, returns, and damage claims. This can be prevented by evaluating requirements and investing in proper equipment and materials.

# Chapter 7

# Maximizing Savings through Proper Evaluation of Packaging and Storage Requirements

**Maximizing Savings through Proper Evaluation of Packaging and Storage Requirements.**

When buying food ingredients, it is important to consider not only the quality and safety of the ingredients themselves but also the packaging and storage requirements necessary to ensure their safety and freshness. Neglecting to evaluate these requirements can result in the sale and distribution of contaminated or expired food, which can cause serious health problems and harm to consumers.

Not evaluating packaging and storage requirements is a common mistake made by businesses, and can have significant consequences for product quality and safety.

- **Product Quality:** Proper packaging and storage can help protect a product from damage, extend its shelf life, and preserve its freshness and flavor. If packaging and storage requirements are not evaluated, products can be damaged during transportation or storage, leading to decreased quality and reduced customer satisfaction.

- **Food Safety:** Food products require specific packaging and storage conditions to prevent the growth of harmful bacteria and other microorganisms that can cause food borne illness. Neglecting to evaluate these requirements can put public health at risk and result in food safety issues.

- **Cost:** Poor packaging and storage can result in increased costs for businesses due to product waste, returns, and damage claims. Evaluating packaging and storage requirements and investing in proper equipment and materials can help reduce these costs and increase overall efficiency.

- **Legal Liability:** Neglecting to evaluate packaging and storage requirements can also result in legal liability for businesses. In the event of a food borne illness outbreak, businesses that did not properly evaluate their packaging and storage requirements may be held responsible and face costly legal fees and penalties.

In conclusion, evaluating packaging and storage requirements is a crucial step in ensuring product quality, food safety, cost-effectiveness, and compliance with legal requirements.

To avoid this, it is essential that food industry players take a proactive and vigilant approach to food packaging and storage. This includes carefully examining the packaging of food ingredients to ensure that it is appropriate for the type of food and that it is designed to keep the food fresh and safe. In addition, food industry players must also ensure that they have in place the necessary storage facilities and equipment, such as refrigerators and freezers, to keep food products at the appropriate temperature and prevent contamination.

Furthermore, food industry players must also be aware of the storage requirements for different types of food ingredients and must ensure that they are stored in the appropriate conditions to maintain their freshness and quality. This includes paying attention to expiration dates and regularly checking for signs of spoilage, such as discoloration, odors, and changes in texture.

Another reason for neglecting packaging and storage requirements is a lack of knowledge about the requirements and their importance.

Many food industry players may not be aware of the appropriate packaging and storage requirements for different types of food ingredients, and may not understand the serious health risks associated with using inappropriate packaging or storage methods. This lack of knowledge can result in serious mistakes, such as storing food ingredients at the wrong temperature, which can cause spoilage and contamination.

In addition to these factors, the food industry is constantly changing, and new packaging and storage requirements are being introduced regularly. This can make it difficult for food industry players to keep up with the latest requirements and may result in the use of outdated or inappropriate packaging and storage methods.

To avoid these problems, it is essential that food industry players take a proactive approach to evaluate packaging and storage requirements, and that they invest in the knowledge and resources needed to ensure that they are meeting the latest requirements. This includes seeking advice from experts in the field, attending training sessions and workshops, and consulting with industry associations and trade organizations.

Food industry players should also take a comprehensive approach to evaluate packaging and storage requirements, considering all factors that may affect the quality, safety, and freshness of the food ingredients, including temperature, humidity, light, and pressure. They should also consider the potential impact of shipping and handling, and should select packaging materials and methods that will provide adequate protection against these factors.

In conclusion, evaluating packaging and storage requirements is a critical aspect of the food industry, and is essential for ensuring the safety and freshness of food ingredients. Food industry players must take a proactive and vigilant approach to these requirements, investing in the knowledge and resources needed to ensure that they are meeting the latest standards, and taking into account all factors that may affect the quality, safety, and freshness of the food ingredients. Failure to evaluate packaging and storage requirements can result in serious consequences for both consumers and the food industry and must be avoided at all costs.

⬮ **MORAL OF CHAPTER** ⬮

---

The moral of the chapter on "Mitigating Risks in Pricing and Supply Chain Management" is to emphasize the importance of considering various factors that can impact pricing and supply chain stability in order to make informed decisions and minimize risks. This includes conducting thorough price and quantity analysis, being aware of external factors that can affect pricing, implementing forex hedging strategies to protect against currency fluctuations, and ensuring the financial stability of suppliers. By paying attention to these factors, businesses can ensure they are making sound decisions that will result in long-term success.

# Chapter 8

# Mitigating Risks in Pricing Decisions: A Comprehensive Approach

## Neglecting the Influence of External Factors on Pricing

**Climate conditions:** The unpredictable weather of late has had a dramatic impact on the prices of food ingredients, particularly produce. In particular, the effects of extreme weather patterns, such as heavy rains, strong winds, and even droughts, have caused the prices of some fruits and vegetables to skyrocket, resulting in a sharp increase in grocery store prices. As a result, many consumers are finding it increasingly difficult to afford essential ingredients for their meals. This situation has been further exacerbated by the global pandemic, which has caused a significant disruption in the supply chain, leading to shortages of certain products. This has caused a further increase in the cost of goods, making it even more difficult for individuals to provide nutritious meals for their families.

By avoiding these mistakes, buyers can save money, get better-quality ingredients, and provide their families with more nutritious meals. Additionally, buyers can save money by buying in-season produce, taking advantage of discounts, and purchasing items directly from the source. By following these simple steps, buyers can ensure they are getting the best value for their money.

Additionally, there are other strategies buyers can employ to save money and get the most out of their food purchases. Look for items that are on sale or buy in bulk when possible. It is also important to compare prices between different stores and look for coupons or discounts that can be applied to food items. Finally, consider buying from local farmers or producers in order to get fresh, organic ingredients, and support the local economy. By arming themselves with the knowledge of common mistakes and the strategies to avoid them, buyers can make smarter decisions and get the most out of their food purchases

It is also important to consider the environmental impact of food purchases. Buying organic produce, for instance, can help reduce the number of pesticides and other chemicals used in food production. Additionally, shopping locally can help support local farmers and reduce the carbon footprint of transporting goods. Furthermore, buying in bulk can be an economical option, as long as buyers make sure to store the products properly and use them up before they expire.

Finally, buyers should take the time to read labels and research ingredients to ensure they are getting the most nutritious food possible.

By following these tips and using common sense, buyers can purchase quality ingredients while also minimizing their environmental impact and saving money.

The recent rainfall patterns have had a significant impact on the prices of food ingredients in many parts of the world. The heavy downpours and flooding have led to a decrease in crop yields, driving up the cost of agricultural inputs. This has, in turn, led to a rise in the prices of food ingredients, making it more expensive for individuals and businesses to purchase the necessary ingredients for their recipes.

Additionally, the increased rainfall has led to the flooding of some farms, causing further losses in the production of food ingredients and thus creating an even greater strain on the availability of ingredients, and further pushing prices up. With the ever-increasing cost of food ingredients, it is becoming increasingly difficult for individuals and businesses alike to afford the necessary ingredients for their recipes.

In such a scenario, it is essential to be aware of the common mistakes made by buyers when purchasing food ingredients. This article will discuss the most common mistakes made by buyers and how to fix them permanently. The mistakes discussed will include the following: failing to compare prices, not checking the quality of ingredients, buying in bulk without considering storage needs, and not researching seasonal availability. We will also discuss how to avoid making these mistakes in the future to ensure that buyers can get the best value for their money when purchasing food ingredients.

To ensure that buyers are getting the best value for their money when purchasing food ingredients, it is important to understand the common mistakes that can be made. Failing to compare prices, not checking the quality of ingredients, buying in bulk without considering storage needs, and not researching seasonal availability are all mistakes that can be avoided with a bit of planning. By comparing prices from different vendors, checking the quality of ingredients, considering storage needs, and researching seasonal availability, buyers can save money and make sure they are buying healthy ingredients.

By comparing prices from different vendors, buyers can get the best value for their money. It is also important to check the quality of ingredients to ensure that the necessary nutrition is being provided. Additionally, buyers should take into account their storage needs before buying in bulk, as this can help them save money in the long run. Lastly, researching seasonal availability can help buyers find the ingredients they need at the lowest possible price. By following these tips, buyers can save money and make sure they are buying healthy ingredients.

## Economic factors

Economic factors are one of the most important driving forces behind price movements in any market. Supply and demand, inflation levels, changes in interest rates, and public sector policies are all factors that can influence prices. Economic factors that impact prices include:

1. **Supply and demand:** The prices of food ingredients are determined by the forces of supply and demand. Supply refers to the amount of a good or service that is available, while demand is the amount of a good or service that people are willing to buy. This relationship between supply and demand affects the prices of food ingredients, as an increase in demand will lead to an increase in price. Conversely, an increase in the supply of food ingredients can lower prices. It is important to note that the prices of food ingredients can also be impacted by other factors, such as the cost of production, transportation, and availability of resources.

2. **Inflation:** The rising cost of living due to inflation is having a drastic effect on the prices

of food ingredients, making it difficult for many people to afford the basic items required for cooking. As a result of inflation, the prices of food staples such as grains, sugar, and other basic produce have been climbing steadily in recent years, leading to a situation where many are struggling to make ends meet. This has been particularly hard on low-income households, who are finding it more difficult than ever to purchase the ingredients they need to prepare meals for their families. The situation is further compounded by the fact that the cost of living is increasing, making it increasingly difficult to make ends meet. It's a situation that is having a serious impact on the ability of many people to access nutritious and affordable meals.

3. **Interest rates:** The cost of living is steadily increasing due to the rise in interest rates. This is having a direct impact on the prices of food ingredients that are needed for everyday meals. Many households are struggling to cope with the increasing costs and it is causing a great deal of financial hardship. Consequently, the demand for cheaper and more economical ingredients is on the rise, with consumers having to find more creative ways to stretch their budgets. This has led to a surge in the number of food suppliers

offering discounted prices, as well as a shift in the types of foods that are being consumed. It has also resulted in the emergence of new and innovative ways to prepare meals, such as using fresh produce and cutting back on processed foods. Ultimately, interest rates are making it more difficult for consumers to afford the ingredients they need, which is having a significant impact on the cost of living.

4. **Currency exchange rates:** Currency exchange rates have a significant impact on the prices of food ingredients around the world. When the rate of one currency against another is less favorable, the cost of the ingredients necessary to create a dish or meal can become prohibitively expensive. This can affect the cost of food items in restaurants, markets, and even grocery stores. The volatility of currency exchange rates can also make it difficult to budget for certain ingredients, as prices may fluctuate dramatically in a short period of time. In addition to the direct impact of exchange rates on the cost of food ingredients, there can also be indirect impacts. For example, if the currency of a given country is weak, imports become more expensive, which can drive up the cost of food ingredients that are sourced from abroad. As a result, it is

important for everyone involved in the food industry to be aware of the impacts of currency exchange rates on the price of food ingredients.

5. **Government policies:** Government policies have a huge impact on the prices of food ingredients, with the cost of certain items rising or falling depending on the measures that have been implemented. For example, if the government introduces a new tax on certain food items, then their price could increase in the short term. On the other hand, subsidies and other forms of financial aid can result in a decrease in the cost of certain food products. In addition, government regulations can also have a significant effect on the prices of food ingredients, as manufacturers and suppliers may be required to adhere to certain requirements that could add to the cost of production. All of these factors can lead to an increase or decrease in the prices of food ingredients, and it is important for businesses and consumers alike to be aware of how government policies can affect the cost of their food.

6. **Raw material costs:** The prices of food ingredients are being driven up due to the increasing cost of raw materials. This is an issue that is affecting businesses across the food

industry, from restaurants to grocery stores. As the cost of raw materials continues to rise, businesses struggle to keep their prices competitive and affordable for consumers. This is resulting in price hikes for food ingredients and is creating a ripple effect that is impacting consumers in many ways. Not only are prices going up, but the quality of food ingredients is also being affected as businesses are forced to make cuts in order to keep costs down. This is a major problem that is having a negative impact on consumers, businesses, and the food industry in general.

7. **Market competition:** The market competition between sellers of food ingredients has become increasingly fierce in recent years, driving prices down to levels that are more competitive than ever. This has resulted in prices of food ingredients becoming more affordable for consumers, while at the same time putting pressure on businesses within the industry as they struggle to remain profitable. Companies are continually developing new strategies to remain competitive in the market and to ensure their prices are competitive. Consumers are also looking for ways to save money, such as taking advantage of sales or finding new sources for

ingredients. As market competition continues to grow, there is no doubt that the prices of food ingredients will continue to be strongly impacted.

8. **Natural disasters:** The prices of food ingredients have been greatly affected by the barrage of natural disasters that have been ravaging our planet in recent years. The destruction of crops, the loss of livestock, and the contamination of water sources have all contributed to the increasing cost of basic food components. This has had a dramatic effect on the cost of food products, leading to a rise in the cost of living for many people. In addition, the disruption of the global food supply chain has made it increasingly difficult for producers to access the ingredients needed for their products, leading to further increases in the cost of food. This has had a significant impact on the economies of many regions around the world, as people are forced to pay more for food than they could previously afford.

## Shipping Line

The rising costs of shipping food ingredients around the world are having a profound effect on the prices of these items. This is due to increasing fuel costs and other expenses associated with transporting these goods, which are making it more expensive for companies to move these items. This is causing a ripple effect on the global market, as the prices of food ingredients are increasing, which in turn is making it more difficult for businesses and consumers to afford these items.

Ignoring shipping costs: Many buyers overlook shipping costs when budgeting for their food ingredients, which can lead to unexpected expenses and delays. To avoid this, always include shipping costs in your budget, and look for suppliers that offer discounts for bulk orders.

This is a major concern, as it could lead to shortages of essential ingredients, potentially impacting the production of food items, and ultimately leading to higher prices for consumers. In order to help consumers and businesses alike avoid these rising costs, it's important to understand the mistakes that are often made when purchasing food ingredients. Here are seven of the most common mistakes that 90% of buyers make when procuring food ingredients, and how to fix them permanently.

**Protect currency fluctuations-Forex Hedging strategy**

**What is Forex Hedging?**

Forex hedging is a risk management strategy used in currency trading to protect against losses from unfavorable exchange rate movements. The basic idea behind hedging is to take an offsetting position in a related currency pair to minimize exposure to price fluctuations. For example, if an investor has a long position in the EUR/USD currency pair and is worried about a potential decline in the value of the euro, they may take a short position in the same currency pair to offset the risk. There are several different forex hedging strategies, including using options, forwards, or currency swaps. The choice of strategy will depend on a variety of factors, including the size of the investment, the investor's risk tolerance, and the time horizon for the investment.

Forex hedging is a strategy that is used by forex traders in order to reduce the risk which is usually associated with the forex market. Most beginners who trade in the forex market are not even aware of forex hedging techniques. But these strategies are used regularly by expert traders to minimize losses. In high-level terms, forex hedging involves selling and buying currency pairs so that they can be protected from fluctuating exchange rates.

The term 'forex hedging' can be thought of as buying a car insurance policy. In the case of car insurance, the policy reduces the cost to be borne by you in case of negative events; still, you cannot be completely covered. Similarly, when you make use of forex hedging strategies, you are covered to some extent but complete protection is not available. Forex hedging protects the long or short position of a currency pair against downside or upside risk.

There are various strategies that are used by forex traders. The most popular among them is the usage of derivatives. The term which is used in the forex market is called a futures contract. This contract is very similar to a normal contract, the only difference being that a currency is being traded instead of a stock. In this contract, there is an agreement to buy or sell the currency at a particular price on a specified date. They work similarly to normal contracts and these provide a very good strategy to hedge against currency rate fluctuations.

One more popular forex method is to use multiple currency pairs. For example, in this strategy, a trader can hold two different currency pairs euros-to-dollars and euros-to-yen. In a euros-to-dollars is facing difficult times, the trader can easily offset the losses by selling the euros-to-yen currency pair. In this case, the short and long positions of the euro occur at the same time and therefore becomes a good hedging strategy.

Some forex traders also use the difference in interest rates as a hedging tool. In this hedging strategy, the traders take positions of the same currency pair with two different brokers. One of these brokers charges some interest while the other one does not. When the market is positive, the trader gains from both traders. But when the market is not favorable for that currency pair, then he will have to pay interest to only one broker while he earns the rollover interest from another broker. Forex hedging should be done by experienced traders only since it can be very confusing for a beginner to the forex market.

## Why is it important?

Forex Hedging is a popular investment strategy used by traders and investors in the foreign exchange market to reduce the risk of currency fluctuations. In this market, traders buy and sell different currencies with the aim of making a profit from the difference in their exchange rates. However, with currency values constantly fluctuating, the market can be highly volatile, making it difficult to predict the value of a currency in the future.

This is where the Forex Hedging strategy comes in. This strategy involves taking out a simultaneous long and short position in two different currencies to offset any losses that may occur due to currency fluctuations. In other words, if the value of one currency decreases, the gains made in the other currency can offset those losses.

Forex Hedging is important because it provides traders and investors with a way to manage their currency risk. By reducing the risk of losses, this strategy helps traders to minimize the impact of currency fluctuations and to focus on making profits from other aspects of the market.

This is particularly important for those who trade frequently or have large positions in the market, as even a small change in currency value can have a significant impact on their bottom line.

Forex Hedging is also important for those who trade in multiple currencies, as it helps to reduce the overall risk of their portfolio. By diversifying their currency exposure, traders can reduce the impact of any one currency's decline on their portfolio. This is particularly important for long-term investors who want to ensure the stability of their investments over time.

In conclusion, Forex Hedging is an important strategy for those looking to reduce their currency risk in the foreign exchange market. By taking out a simultaneous long and short position in two different currencies, traders and investors can offset any losses and minimize the impact of currency fluctuations on their portfolios. Whether you are a frequent trader or a long-term investor, the Forex Hedging strategy is a valuable tool to help you manage your currency risk and ensure the stability of your investments over time.

**How to Stay Protected?**

Forex (foreign exchange) fluctuation can pose a risk to individuals and businesses that engage in international trade or have financial assets in foreign currencies. To stay protected from forex fluctuations, you can follow these steps:

- **Hedge with financial instruments:** You can use financial instruments, such as currency forward contracts or options, to hedge against forex fluctuations. This involves locking in an exchange rate for a future transaction, reducing your exposure to market volatility.

- **Diversify currency holdings:** Diversifying your currency holdings across different countries can reduce your exposure to currency fluctuations in a single market.

- **Monitor market trends:** Regularly monitoring market trends and being aware of potential risks and opportunities can help you make informed decisions about currency exposure.

- **Use hedging strategies in investment portfolios:** If you have investment portfolios, consider using hedging strategies, such as currency-hedged exchange-traded funds, to reduce exposure to currency fluctuations.

- **Work with a financial advisor:** Working with a financial advisor who has expertise in forex markets can help you develop a comprehensive risk management strategy that fits your specific needs.

It is important to note that there are no guaranteed methods for protecting against forex fluctuations, and all investments carry some degree of risk. It's always best to consult with a financial advisor before making investment decisions.

## Financial Stability of supplier

Financial stability is a critical factor in the selection and management of suppliers, as it directly impacts a company's ability to secure the materials and services it needs to operate effectively. By considering the financial stability of a supplier, companies can minimize the risk of supplier failure and ensure a stable and reliable supply chain.

There are several reasons why the financial stability of a supplier is important:

1. **Protects against supplier bankruptcy:** The financial stability of a supplier is a key indicator of their ability to meet their obligations, including delivering goods and services on time and at the agreed-upon price. By choosing a financially

stable supplier, companies can reduce the risk of supplier bankruptcy and the related costs and disruptions.

2. **Ensures timely delivery of goods:** Suppliers that are in financial distress are more likely to experience delays in delivering goods, which can have a negative impact on a company's operations and customer satisfaction. Financial stability of suppliers ensures that they have the resources to invest in their operations, maintain high-quality standards, and meet delivery schedules.

3. **Increases bargaining power:** Companies that work with financially stable suppliers are often in a stronger bargaining position when negotiating prices and terms. Suppliers that are in a stable financial position are less likely to compromise on quality or delivery times to meet price demands.

4. **Minimizes the risk of price spikes:** Suppliers that are in financial distress are more likely to raise their prices in order to remain afloat, which can negatively impact a company's bottom line. By selecting financially stable suppliers, companies can minimize the risk of unexpected price spikes and maintain a more predictable cost structure.

5. **Supports long-term relationships:** Working with financially stable suppliers helps to foster long-term relationships, as both parties can rely on a stable and consistent supply of goods and services. This supports better planning and forecasting, reduces the risk of supply chain disruptions, and enhances overall efficiency.

   Credibility checking of suppliers is an important step in the process of sourcing goods or services.

   Here are some steps you can follow to assess the credibility of a supplier:

6. **Research the company:** Start by researching the supplier's business, its history, and reputation. Look for reviews and ratings online, and check its website and social media profiles.

7. **Check industry associations:** If the supplier is a member of any industry associations, such as chambers of commerce or trade organizations, check their credibility and reputation.

8. **Verify credentials:** Ensure that the supplier has the necessary licenses, certifications, and accreditations for the goods or services it provides.

9. **Evaluate financial stability:** Check the supplier's financial stability by reviewing its financial statements and credit reports.

10. **Contact references:** Contact the supplier's previous clients and ask about their experiences.

11. **On-site inspection:** Visit the supplier's facilities to assess its operations, including its manufacturing processes, quality control systems, and storage facilities.

12. **Negotiate terms:** Establish clear terms and conditions in a contract, including payment terms, delivery schedules, and warranties.

By following these steps, you can reduce the risk of doing business with unreliable suppliers and ensure that you receive high-quality goods and services.

In conclusion, financial stability is a critical factor in the selection and management of suppliers, and companies that prioritize this in their supplier selection and management processes can reduce the risk of supplier failure, ensure a stable and reliable supply chain, and improve overall operational efficiency and profitability.

MORAL OF CHAPTER

The moral of this chapter is that effective inventory management is crucial for the success of any business, and it involves a multitude of interrelated factors. Understanding the shelf life of ingredients and ensuring their timely replenishment is essential for preserving product quality. Additionally, having adequate warehousing space for buffer stocks is important for ensuring the continuity of supply and maintaining customer satisfaction. By monitoring and updating the status of both fast and slow moving inventory on a regular basis, businesses can stay ahead of the curve and respond quickly to changes in demand. Furthermore, conducting monthly updates on pending volumes can help keep track of inventory levels and prevent stock shortages or overstocking.

# Chapter 9

# The importance of Shelf Life of Ingredients

## Shelf Life of Ingredients: The Importance of Understanding it for Food Manufacturers

As a food manufacturer, it is essential to understand the shelf life of the ingredients you use in your products. Shelf life refers to the length of time a product can be stored and still maintain its quality, safety, and nutritional value. Not fully comprehending the shelf life of ingredients can have significant consequences for your business, including waste, decreased quality, and even health issues. In this article, we will explore the dangers of not understanding the shelf life of ingredients and provide tips for ensuring that you buy ingredients that are fresh, safe, and of the highest quality.

Not understanding the shelf life of ingredients is a common mistake that can have significant consequences for food businesses. Some of the problems caused by not understanding the shelf life of ingredients include:

1. **Food waste:** Using ingredients that have gone past their shelf life can result in food waste, as the ingredients may no longer be safe to use or may not meet quality standards.

2. **Food safety concerns:** Ingredients that have gone past their shelf life can pose a food safety risk, as they may contain harmful bacteria or other microorganisms that can cause food borne illness.

3. **Reduced product quality:** Ingredients that have gone past their shelf life may not have the same taste, texture, or appearance as fresh ingredients, which can reduce the overall quality of the final product.

4. **Increased costs:** Replacing wasted ingredients and dealing with food safety issues can increase costs for a business, reducing its profitability.

To avoid these problems, it is important for food businesses to understand the shelf life of their ingredients and properly store and manage their inventory to ensure that they are using fresh and safe ingredients in their products. This can help to reduce waste, improve product quality, and ensure food safety.

Not fully understanding the shelf life of ingredients can have several negative consequences for food manufacturers. Firstly, it can result in decreased quality and lower customer satisfaction. When ingredients are past their shelf life, they can become dry, stale, or rancid, which can change the flavor and texture of your products. This can lead to negative reviews and a decrease in repeat customers.

Additionally, not understanding the shelf life of ingredients can result in waste. If you purchase ingredients that are close to their expiration date, you may not be able to use them all before they go bad, which means that you'll have to throw them away. This results in waste and a decrease in profits.

Finally, not understanding the shelf life of ingredients can also have an impact on the safety of your products. Some ingredients, like raw meats and dairy products, can become contaminated with bacteria like E. coli or Salmonella if they're stored for too long. This can cause food poisoning, which can have serious consequences for your business, including legal action and a loss of consumer trust.

**Tips for Buying Fresh, Safe, and High-Quality Ingredients.**

To ensure that you buy ingredients that are fresh, safe, and of the highest quality, there are a few tips that you can follow. These include:

5. **Read the Label:** When buying for ingredients, be sure to read the label carefully. Most labels will indicate the best-by date, which is the date that the product is expected to be at its best quality. Try to purchase ingredients with a later best-by date to ensure that they have a longer shelf life. Be sure to check the ingredients, nutrition facts, and any warnings or cautions that may be provided. This can help you make an informed decision about which product is right for you and your needs. Additionally, it is wise to look for labels that provide information about the origin of the product and if the item is organic or sustainably sourced. Paying attention to labels can be a great way to ensure that you are purchasing a product that is both safe and of high quality. Furthermore, reading the label can help you to identify any potential allergies or sensitivities that you may have to certain ingredients.

6. **Look for Proper Packaging:** Proper packaging can help extend the shelf life of food ingredients.

For example, vacuum-sealed packaging can help prevent air and moisture from entering and causing spoilage. When sending or receiving something, it is absolutely essential to use the right kind of packaging. Using the wrong packaging can lead to irreparable damage to the item, which could not only cost you money but also time and effort. This is why it is so important to choose the right type of packaging that is suitable for the item in question and its fragility. Doing research on different types of packaging and testing them out is a great way to make sure that the item is protected during transport and arrives safely. Failing to take the necessary precautions can result in a costly mistake.

7. **Work with Reliable Suppliers:** Work with suppliers who have a proven track record of providing high-quality, fresh ingredients. Consider visiting the supplier's facility to see how they handle and store their products. Working with reliable suppliers is essential in any business, as they are the ones who provide goods and services that are important to the success of your company. Having a good relationship with your suppliers is key, as it ensures that you receive quality products and services on time and at a competitive price. It's

important to take the time to research the background of potential suppliers and to make sure you are getting reliable services. Consider asking for references from other businesses that have used the supplier, as well as looking at their past performance and customer reviews. You should also make sure that your suppliers are familiar with the standards and regulations that apply to your industry. Taking the time to establish a good relationship with reliable suppliers can pay off in the long run and ensure that your business runs smoothly and efficiently.

8. **Store Ingredients Properly:** Once you've purchased your ingredients, be sure to store them properly. Store perishable ingredients like dairy and meat in the refrigerator, and be sure to follow proper food storage guidelines to prevent contamination and spoilage. It is important to store ingredients properly in order to maintain their freshness and quality. Make sure to keep all items in their original, unopened packaging, if possible. If needed, transfer items to airtight containers or resealable bags. Store items away from direct heat and light, and in a cool, dry environment. Refrigerate or freeze items such as dairy, eggs, and meats. If items are stored in the refrigerator, make sure they

are labeled and placed in the proper section of the fridge. Additionally, it is important to check expiration dates and discard any items that have passed their expiration. Keeping ingredients in the proper storage environment will ensure they are fresh and safe to use.

9. **Monitor Shelf Life:** Finally, be sure to monitor the shelf life of your ingredients and use them in a timely manner. This will help prevent waste and ensure that your products are of the highest quality. Monitoring the shelf life of products is an essential part of managing any business. Knowing when a product needs to be replaced can improve efficiency and prevent unnecessary waste. It also helps to ensure that customers receive the highest quality product possible. Taking the time to track the shelf life of items can also help businesses to develop better ordering and stocking practices. By understanding the shelf life of products, businesses can decide how much inventory to keep on hand and how often to place orders. This can lead to improved customer satisfaction and fewer delays due to out of stock items. In addition, understanding the shelf life of products can also help businesses to create more accurate pricing models and reduce losses due to expired

products. Keeping a close eye on shelf life can be beneficial for any business.

In conclusion, as a food manufacturer, understanding the shelf life of ingredients is crucial for ensuring that your products are fresh, safe, and of the highest quality. By following the tips outlined in this article, you can reduce waste, improve quality, and prevent food-related health issues. By doing so, you'll not only ensure the success of your business but also the satisfaction of your customers.

**Ensuring Continuity of Supply:** The Importance of Warehousing for buffer stocks.

Warehousing of suppliers is an essential part of the supply chain, as it ensures that goods are stored safely until they are needed. It is important to have an effective warehousing system in place that is able to efficiently store, manage, and distribute goods to customers. Warehousing is also important for inventory control and management, as it provides a secure storage area for all of the products that are being supplied. Proper warehousing can help to keep track of inventory levels and allow for quick distribution of goods when needed.

Additionally, warehouses can also be used for temperature control, which is especially important for perishable goods. Furthermore, warehousing can provide customers with quick delivery of their orders, as well as flexibility in fulfilling orders with shorter lead times. All of these factors make warehousing an important part of the supply chain and one that should not be overlooked. The goal of supplier warehousing is to improve supply chain efficiency, reduce costs, and increase customer satisfaction by providing quick and reliable access to products.

Warehousing of suppliers refers to the process of storing and managing goods and products on behalf of a supplier. This typically involves receiving and organizing the products, monitoring inventory levels, and preparing the products for shipment to customers.

**Temperature Control**

Temperature regulation is a key factor in many processes and applications. The ability to accurately and effectively monitor and adjust temperatures is essential for ensuring that operations run smoothly. Temperature control systems use a variety of techniques to measure and adjust temperatures, such as thermocouples, thermistors, and RTDs. These sensors detect changes in temperature and then adjust the output accordingly. Temperature control systems can also be used in combination with other controls, such as flow or pressure, to regulate both the temperature and other parameters.

Additionally, temperature control systems can be used to maintain a stable temperature within a certain range in order to keep the process running optimally. Temperature control systems are used in a variety of industries, including manufacturing, food production, and pharmaceuticals. They are an invaluable tool for ensuring product quality and safety, as well as providing a comfortable environment for workers. Temperature control in warehousing is important to maintain the quality and safety of perishable goods and products that are sensitive to temperature changes. It involves maintaining a consistent and controlled temperature environment to prevent spoilage, degradation, or damage to the stored items.

This may include using temperature-controlled storage areas, refrigeration or air conditioning systems, and monitoring devices to ensure that the temperature remains within specified ranges. Proper temperature control can help extend the shelf life of products, improve product quality, and reduce waste and spoilage, ultimately leading to cost savings and improved customer satisfaction.

## GMP

GMP stands for "Good Manufacturing Practices". It is a set of guidelines and standards for the production, control, and storage of pharmaceuticals, medical devices, and food products. The goal of GMP is to ensure that these products are of high quality and meet safety and efficacy standards. These regulations are established by the government and enforced by regulatory authorities. GMPs apply to all aspects of production and processing, from raw materials to finished products. They cover areas such as quality control and assurance, product testing, product handling and storage, packaging and labeling, and employee training and safety.

GMPs provide a framework for manufacturers to adhere to in order to ensure that products are produced in a safe and reliable manner that meets the quality standards set by the government. GMPs are also important for protecting consumers from products that may be contaminated or otherwise dangerous. Adhering to GMPs helps to promote confidence in products and ensure that all products, from food and drugs to cosmetics and medical devices, are safe for consumers to use.

Adherence to GMP is mandatory for companies involved in these industries to maintain public trust and protect the health of consumers. GMP covers all aspects of production from the raw materials, premises, and equipment to the training and personal hygiene of staff. The goal of GMP is to minimize the risks involved in the production process that cannot be eliminated through testing the final product. Adherence to GMP regulations helps to ensure that the products are of high quality and safe for human consumption.

## Docking Undocking

Docking and undocking a vessel is a complex and delicate operation, requiring a great deal of skill and precision. It involves the careful maneuvering of the vessel into the necessary position, ensuring that it is properly aligned and connected to the dockside. The ship must be carefully secured and all safety protocols must be followed to ensure a safe and successful operation. Once securely docked, the process of unloading and loading cargo and personnel can begin. Undocking is just as complicated as docking, requiring a thorough knowledge of the vessel's capabilities and limitations, as well as the ability to make quick and accurate decisions.

The vessel must be carefully and slowly maneuvered away from the dockside and out of the harbor. It is essential to take into account factors such as water depths, currents and wind conditions to ensure a safe and successful undocking.

Once the vessel is successfully docked and unloaded, the buyers must take care to properly store and handle the food ingredients. Poor storage conditions, such as exposure to sunlight, high temperatures, and humidity, can significantly reduce the shelf life of the food ingredients and make them unusable.

Furthermore, improper handling and transportation of food ingredients can cause contamination and food poisoning. To prevent these problems from occurring, buyers should use the proper packaging and labeling for their food ingredients and ensure that they are stored and handled in the proper environment. Additionally, buyers should be aware of the expiration date of their food ingredients and take steps to replace them before they become unusable.

**Handling Fast and Slow Moving Inventory in Inventory Management.**

Fast-moving goods are that move quickly are often in high demand. They are sought after for their convenience and speed of delivery. Quick-moving goods are often more expensive than slower-moving goods, but they can be worth the extra cost due to their timely arrival.

Slow-moving goods are that move slowly. It's important to pay attention to the goods that move slowly in your inventory. Keeping too much of these can cause a cash flow issue, which can be detrimental to the success of your F&B empire. Consider eliminating or reducing the slow-moving items to help with cost savings.

Fast-moving goods and slow-moving goods are two different categories of inventory items, and understanding the difference between them is important for effective inventory management. Fast-moving goods are items that are sold quickly, while slow-moving goods are items that take a longer time to sell.

Calculating fast-moving goods and slow-moving goods involves analyzing the sales history of each inventory item to determine its velocity or the rate at which it is sold. This information can be used to prioritize inventory management decisions and to make informed decisions about stock levels, pricing, and marketing strategies.

To calculate fast-moving goods, the number of units sold during a specified time period (such as a month or a quarter) is divided by the total number of units of the item that were available for sale during that same time period. The resulting number is the velocity of the item.

Items with high velocities are considered fast-moving goods, while items with low velocities are considered slow-moving goods. The importance of analyzing fast-moving goods and slow-moving goods is that it provides a basis for making informed decisions about inventory management, such as deciding which items to stock more heavily and which items to phase out.

Another important metric for effective inventory management is average inventory turns, which measure the number of times the average inventory is sold and replaced over a specified period of time (such as a year). A higher average inventory turns number indicates that inventory is being sold and replaced quickly, while a lower average inventory turns number indicates that inventory is not moving as quickly.

It is important to calculate and analyze fast-moving goods, slow-moving goods, and average inventory turns regularly to ensure that inventory management strategies are aligned with business goals and to minimize the risk of stockouts, overstocking, and obsolescence. This helps to improve overall efficiency and profitability and to provide a more stable and predictable supply chain.

## Monthly update for pending volumes

### The Importance of Monthly Contract Updates for Buyers

In today's fast-paced business environment, staying on top of your contracts is more important than ever. Regular contract updates can help you ensure that your agreements remain relevant and in line with current market conditions. Here are a few reasons why monthly contract updates are essential for buyers:

1. **Price Changes:** Monthly contract updates can help you stay on top of any changes in the prices of goods and services. If the market price of a product or service changes, your contract should reflect that change. By updating your contracts on a monthly basis, you can ensure that you are paying the correct price for the goods or services you receive.

2. **Volume Changes:** Monthly contract updates can also help you manage any changes in the volume of goods or services you receive. For example, if you need to increase or decrease the amount of a product you purchase, your contract should reflect that change. Monthly contract updates can help you keep your agreements in line with your current needs.

3. **Delivery Changes:** Monthly contract updates can also help you manage any changes in the delivery schedule for goods or services. If the delivery schedule for a product changes, your contract should reflect that change. Monthly contract updates can help you stay on top of any changes in the delivery schedule and ensure that you receive the goods or services you need when you need them.

4. **Terms and Conditions Changes:** Finally, monthly contract updates can help you stay on

top of any changes in the terms and conditions of your contracts. For example, if the warranty period for a product changes, your contract should reflect that change. Monthly contract updates can help you stay on top of any changes in the terms and conditions of your contracts and ensure that you are protected in the event of any disputes.

In conclusion, monthly contract updates are essential for buyers in today's fast-paced business environment. Regular contract updates can help you stay on top of any changes in the prices of goods and services, the volume of goods or services you receive, the delivery schedule for goods or services, and the terms and conditions of your contracts. By updating your contracts on a monthly basis, you can ensure that your agreements remain relevant and in line with current market conditions, which can help you reduce costs, manage risk, and achieve your goals more effectively.

The moral of the chapter is a practice that is becoming increasingly important for the future of our planet. Companies are beginning to realize that investing in sustainable sourcing for food not only helps to reduce their environmental impact, but also provides them with a competitive advantage. Sustainable sourcing for food can include sourcing food from local producers, using renewable energy, reducing food waste, and using sustainable packaging. By investing in sustainable sourcing for food, businesses are helping to ensure that future generations will have access to the same resources that we have access to today. It is a practice that is becoming a vital part of the food industry and one that businesses should strive to invest in.

Chapter 10

# Sustainable sourcing
# for Food Business

## Not Considering Sustainability and Environmental Impact

The production and transportation of certain ingredients can contribute to greenhouse gas emissions, deforestation, and other forms of environmental degradation. It can contribute to deforestation, habitat loss, soil degradation, water pollution, and air pollution, among other issues.

Factors to consider include the origin of the ingredient, methods of production, packaging and transportation, and disposal or recycling of waste. For example, locally sourced and organic ingredients have a smaller carbon footprint compared to those produced and transported from far distances.

Over-exploitation of natural resources can lead to their depletion, which can harm ecosystems and cause loss of biodiversity.

Additionally, ingredients produced through sustainable farming practices, such as reduced use of pesticides and fertilizers, can help protect wildlife and ecosystems. Choosing environmentally friendly packaging, such as biodegradable or recyclable options, can also help reduce waste. By being mindful of these factors, we can work towards a more sustainable food system and preserve the health of our planet for future generations.

It can also contribute to the over-fishing of oceans and the depletion of fish populations, as well as the use of harmful chemicals and pesticides that can harm wildlife and human health. By being mindful of the environmental impact of the ingredients we buy, we can help protect the planet and ensure a sustainable future for all.

It's important to be mindful of these issues and make choices that minimize harm to the environment. This can include choosing locally-sourced and organic ingredients or supporting companies that have environmentally-friendly practices.

**Choose a Reliable Partner**

A strategic partner is important as they bring several benefits to a company, including:

1. Access to new markets, customers, and resources

2. Improved competitiveness and innovation

3. Shared risk and increased efficiency

4. Enhanced credibility and reputation

5. Access to knowledge and expertise

6. Increased financial stability and funding opportunities

Having a strategic partner can help a company achieve its goals faster and more effectively than going it alone. It also allows for a stronger alliance and a better chance of success in a rapidly changing business environment.

**The Importance of Developing Strategic Partners for Purchase versus Vendors.**

In today's fast-paced business environment, companies are constantly looking for ways to streamline their operations and reduce costs. One way to do this is by developing strategic partners for purchase instead of relying solely on vendors. A strategic partner is a company that works closely with you to understand your business needs and provide solutions that help you achieve your goals. In contrast, a vendor is simply a company that sells you a product or service. In this article, we will explore the benefits of developing strategic partners for purchase and why it's important for companies to make this shift.

7. **Improved Communication and Collaboration:** One of the biggest benefits of developing strategic partners for purchase is improved communication and collaboration. With a strategic partner, you have a dedicated team of experts who are committed to understanding your business and working with you to find the best solutions. This level of collaboration can lead to better decision-making, increased efficiency, and improved outcomes.

8. **Access to Expertise and Best Practices:** Another benefit of having a strategic partner for purchase is access to their expertise and best practices. Strategic partners bring a wealth of knowledge and experience to the table, which can help you overcome challenges and find new opportunities. By working closely with a strategic partner, you can learn from their experience and incorporate their best practices into your own operations.

9. **Improved Flexibility and Responsiveness:** Vendors are often focused on selling their products and services, rather than being responsive to your needs. On the other hand, a strategic partner is focused on your success and will work with you to find solutions that meet your unique requirements. This level of flexibility

and responsiveness can help you make decisions quickly and respond to changes in your market or industry more effectively.

10. **Better Cost Management:** Working with a strategic partner for purchase can also lead to better cost management. Strategic partners are committed to finding the best solutions at the right price, which can help you reduce costs and increase profits. In addition, by working closely with a strategic partner, you can negotiate better pricing and terms, which can help you control costs over the long term.

11. **Increased Competitive Advantage:** Finally, having a strategic partner for purchase can help you gain a competitive advantage. By working closely with a strategic partner, you can access the latest technologies, products, and services that can help you differentiate yourself from your competitors. This can give you a significant advantage in your market and help you achieve your business goals.

# Conclusion

In conclusion, the benefits of developing strategic partners for purchase instead of relying solely on vendors are clear. Improved communication and collaboration, access to expertise and best practices, improved flexibility and responsiveness, better cost management, and increased competitive advantage are just a few of the many benefits that companies can realize by making this shift. By developing strong relationships with strategic partners, companies can improve their operations, reduce costs, and achieve their goals more effectively.

## Owner driven company

Owner-driven companies and multinational corporations (MNCs) are two distinct types of businesses with different characteristics and approaches to conducting business. Here is a comparison of the two, along with some of the myths and advantages of working with family-owned businesses.

Myths about family-owned businesses:

1. **Family-owned businesses are not professional:** This is a common misconception. Family-owned businesses can be just as professional and competent as any other type of business.

2. **Family businesses are not innovative:** Family-owned businesses can be just as innovative as other businesses and often have a strong commitment to their customers and community.

3. **Standardized processes:** We always think that MNCs often have established and standardized processes for doing business, which can provide consistency and reliability to customers. But with times Family owned businesses have adopted similar standardized processes.

Advantages of working with family-owned businesses:

1. **Personalized service:** Family-owned businesses often have a more personal approach to doing business and can offer customized solutions to meet the needs of their customers.

2. **Strong values:** Family-owned businesses often have a strong set of values that guide their operations and decision-making.

3. **Responsiveness:** Family-owned businesses are often more responsive to customer needs and can make decisions more quickly than larger corporations.

4. **Local impact:** Family-owned businesses often have a strong impact on the local community and economy, and can provide valuable support to other local businesses.

5. **Direct management approach:** Family-owned businesses often have a flat organizational structure, allowing for direct communication and decision-making with the owners or top management.

6. **Fast action:** Family-owned businesses can often respond quickly to customer needs and changes in the market, allowing for fast and efficient problem-solving.

7. **Lean management:** Family-owned businesses often have a lean management structure, which can result in lower overhead costs and a focus on cost-effectiveness.

8. **Low-cost working:** Due to their smaller size and leaner operations, family-owned businesses may be able to offer lower prices or more competitive pricing compared to larger corporations.

Ultimately, the choice between working with a family-owned business or an MNC will depend on the specific needs and goals of the customer. It is important to carefully evaluate the strengths and weaknesses of each type of business to determine the best fit.

**Debunking the Dependence on COA:** The Distinction between Functional and Nutritional Ingredients.

The dependence on a Certificate of Authenticity (COA) as a measure of authenticity for products and collectibles is a common perception, but it is not necessarily a myth. While a COA can serve as a document that provides proof of authenticity, it is important to note that it is not always a guarantee. There are instances where COAs have been falsified or forged, making it crucial to take additional steps to verify the authenticity of a product or collectible.

It's important to keep in mind that a COA is only as valuable as the credibility of the issuing organization. For example, a COA from a well-respected organization in the industry can carry significant weight, while one from an unknown or untrustworthy source may not be worth much at all.

Ultimately, the best way to ensure the authenticity of a product or collectible is to do your research, consult with experts in the field, and use multiple sources of information to make an informed decision.

While COAs are not always required, they play a crucial role in ensuring product quality and safety. In many cases, customers, regulators, and industry standards require COAs as a way to verify product quality and to protect the health and safety of consumers.

However, it is also true that COAs alone do not guarantee product quality, and that other factors such as manufacturing practices, storage conditions, and distribution channels can also have an impact on product quality. In these cases, a COA serves as only one aspect of a larger quality control process.

In conclusion, while dependency on a COA is not a myth, it is also important to understand that COAs are just one aspect of a larger quality control process, and that other factors can also play a role in ensuring product quality and safety.

Functional and nutritional ingredients are two different types of ingredients used in the food and beverage industry.

Functional ingredients are added to a product for a specific purpose, such as improving texture, preserving freshness, or adding flavor. Examples of functional ingredients include stabilizers, emulsifiers, gums, and thickeners. These ingredients play a crucial role in determining the quality, texture, and stability of a product, and are often essential for the production of certain types of food and beverages. Examples of functional ingredients include stabilizers, emulsifiers, gums, and thickeners.

Nutritional ingredients, on the other hand, are added to a product to provide specific health benefits, or to fortify a product with essential nutrients. Examples of nutritional ingredients include vitamins, minerals, fiber, and protein. These ingredients can help to improve the nutritional profile of a product and can be used to target specific health concerns, such as heart health or weight management. These ingredients can help to improve the nutritional profile of a product and can be used to target specific health concerns, such as heart health or weight management. Examples of nutritional ingredients include vitamins, minerals, fiber, and protein.

Both functional and nutritional ingredients are important components of many food and beverage products, and are carefully selected and regulated by food scientists, nutritionists, and regulatory agencies to ensure that they are safe and effective for their intended purposes.

It is important to note that some ingredients can serve both functional and nutritional roles, depending on the specific product and the intended use. For instance, calcium can be added to a product for both its ability to improve texture and to provide a source of calcium for the consumer. As such, food scientists, nutritionists, and regulatory agencies must carefully select and regulate the ingredients used in food and beverage products to ensure that they are safe and effective for their intended purposes. In short, functional and nutritional ingredients are both important components of many food and beverage products, each playing a distinct role in the production and processing of these products.

In conclusion, functional and nutritional ingredients are two different types of ingredients used in the food and beverage industry, with different roles and purposes in the production and processing of food and beverage products.

**Fixing the Mistakes Permanently:** Implementing a Systematic Approach.

Implementing a systematic approach to corrections and preventative measures is an essential part of successful problem-solving. It requires an organized and comprehensive approach, one that establishes and follows set procedures for identifying, recording, and resolving mistakes. Such a system should be in place before any errors occur so that it can be put into action immediately when needed. This system should be designed to cover all aspects of the problem, from the initial identification of the mistake to the development of solutions and the implementation of corrective actions. The system should be regularly reviewed and updated to ensure that it remains effective and that any changes needed as the problem evolves are taken into account.

Additionally, it should be supported by a documented process, with clear instructions and guidance, so that everyone involved can understand how to use it. With a well-designed and well-executed system in place, mistakes can be identified and corrected quickly, and future problems avoided.

**To implement a systematic approach, follow these steps:**

1. **Define the problem or objective:** It's important to take the time to properly define and understand the issue so that you can determine the best course of action. Doing this can help save time and resources in the long run, as it can prevent you from heading in the wrong direction. Additionally, having a clear understanding of the desired outcome can help provide direction and clarity throughout the process. Defining the problem or objective is a key step in ensuring a successful outcome. Once the problem or objective is clearly defined, it is important to

consider the potential solutions. There are a variety of different solutions available, so it is important to identify the most effective and efficient one. This is best done through research and exploration of the different options, and by considering the pros and cons of each. Taking the time to properly evaluate the solutions available can help ensure that you are making the best decision for the project or endeavor. Additionally, it can help save time, money, and resources in the long run.

2. **Conduct a thorough analysis:** Take the time to conduct a comprehensive and exhaustive analysis. Be sure to evaluate all the relevant data and assess all the possible outcomes before making a final conclusion. Pay close attention to the details, and use all of the available resources to ensure that you have the best understanding of the situation at hand. By taking the time to conduct a thorough analysis, you can be sure that your decisions will be based on the most accurate information available. The next step is to make sure you have a comprehensive understanding of the market. Gather as much information as possible about the industry, the current trends, and the competition. This will help you to identify the

best possible courses of action and identify any potential pitfalls. Additionally, it is important to understand the needs of the customer and what they are looking for to ensure that the product you are offering meets their needs. Finally, consider the pricing of the product and make sure that it is competitive in the market.

3.  **Develop a Plan:** Developing a plan is essential for success. It is important to have a clear idea of what you want to achieve and how you plan to get there. Taking the time to research and come up with the best plan for your particular situation will help you stay focused and motivated to reach your goals. It is also important to be realistic and flexible with your plan, as unexpected changes may occur that require adjustments. It is also beneficial to create milestones and track your progress as you move forward in order to stay on track and make any necessary adjustments or modifications. Having a well-crafted plan in place will help you stay organized and motivated as you work towards achieving your goals. It is also beneficial to create a budget to ensure that you are not spending more than you can afford on food ingredients. This budget should include all of the necessary ingredients as well as any costs

associated with shipping, storage, and other related expenses. Additionally, it is important to read reviews and research different products to make sure you are getting the best quality ingredients for your budget. Finally, make sure to compare prices from different vendors to get the best deal and ensure that you are buying the highest quality ingredients at the best price.

4. **Implement the Plan:** Now that the plan has been formulated, it is time to put it into action. Implementing the plan requires careful consideration and planning. Every step must be thoughtfully considered and executed in order to ensure the success of the plan. The implementation process should begin by setting goals and objectives for the plan, then progress to making sure the resources are available to achieve those goals. This includes ensuring that any necessary personnel, materials, and technology are in place and ready to be utilized. Next, it is important to identify any potential risks that may arise during the implementation of the plan. Once these risks have been identified, strategies can be developed to mitigate them.

Once the implementation process has been completed, it is important to look back and evaluate the plan to ensure it was successful.

This evaluation should include an assessment of the goals that were set, the resources that were used, and the effectiveness of any risk mitigation strategies. It is also important to consider any changes that could be made to improve the plan in the future. After the evaluation is complete, any necessary changes should be made and the plan should be implemented again to ensure it is still achieving the desired results. With proper evaluation and execution, the plan can be a great success and help buyers purchase food ingredients in a more effective and efficient manner.

Finally, the plan should be monitored and evaluated regularly to ensure it is being implemented correctly and achieving the desired results. With careful implementation and monitoring, the plan can be successfully implemented and can bring great success.

5. **Put the plan into action:** To ensure that the plan is put into action, it is essential to have a clear strategy in place and to make sure that everyone involved is fully aware of their responsibilities. Allowing for enough time to carry out the plan, setting achievable goals and objectives, and making sure that the plan is flexible enough to be adapted as necessary, will

all help to ensure that the plan is successful. Taking the time to evaluate and review the plan regularly is another crucial step in making sure that the plan is implemented as intended, and that any necessary changes can be made quickly. By following these steps, the plan can be put into action effectively and efficiently.

Once the plan is in motion, it is important to monitor its progress and check that it is being implemented correctly. This can be done by regularly reviewing the plan, as well as assessing the results of any changes that have been made. It is also important to take into account any feedback from customers or stakeholders, as this can help to further improve the plan and ensure that its objectives are being met. Finally, it is essential to communicate the progress of the plan to all those involved, in order to provide them with the necessary motivation to keep up their efforts.

6. **Evaluate the results:** Analyze the outcomes and assess their significance, taking into consideration the amount of effort and resources expended in the process. Consider the potential implications of the results and how they may affect future decisions and initiatives. Take into account any lessons that can be learned from

the results and how they could be applied in other similar contexts. Ultimately, evaluate the results to gain a better understanding of their impact and decide whether they merit further exploration or additional resources.

Identify ways to improve or optimize the process, such as introducing new techniques or technologies, or making changes to the workflow. Determine the best practices that should be enforced in order to avoid similar mistakes in the future. Develop a plan of action that outlines the steps taken to address the mistakes and ensure that they are not repeated. Finally, track and monitor the progress of the plan to determine whether or not it is having the desired effect.

## Continuously monitor and evaluate the results

Continuously monitor and evaluate the results of your efforts, making sure that they are producing the desired outcomes. Keep track of what has been successful and what has not, and make adjustments as needed to maximize the efficiency of your efforts. Analyze the effectiveness of the strategies you have implemented and identify any areas that could be improved. Take into consideration any feedback you receive from stakeholders, and use it to inform future decisions. Consider if any changes need to be made in terms of resources, processes, or personnel in order to ensure that the desired outcomes are achieved.

Reflect on the resources you have available and identify any gaps that exist in order to better achieve the desired results. Make sure to use a comprehensive assessment process in order to ensure that the results are accurate and reliable. This assessment should include the collection of data, the analysis of data, the identification of trends and patterns, and the completion of a thorough review of the results in order to form conclusions and make recommendations for improvement.

Additionally, create a system for tracking the results of your efforts over time, so that you can identify any areas of improvement and make necessary adjustments to ensure the best possible outcomes.

By following a systematic approach, you can increase the efficiency and effectiveness of your efforts and achieve your goals in a structured and organized manner.

**Notes:**

**Notes:**

## Notes:

**Notes: